Museum of Modern Art/Film Stills Archive

Roman
POLANSKI

a guide to
references and resources

A
Reference
Guide
in
Film
Ronald Gottesman
Editor

Roman
POLANSKI

a guide to
references and resources

GRETCHEN BISPLINGHOFF
VIRGINIA WRIGHT WEXMAN

G.K.HALL&CO.
70 LINCOLN STREET, BOSTON, MASS.

Distributed in the United Kingdom and Europe by George Prior Associated
Publishers Ltd., 37–41 Bedford Row, London W. C. 1 England.

Library of Congress Cataloging in Publication Data

Bisplinghoff, Gretchen.
 Roman Polanski, a guide to references and resources.

 (A Reference publication in film)
 Includes index.
 1. Polanski, Roman—Bibliography.   2. Moving pictures—Plots, themes,
etc.   I. Wexman, Virginia Wright, joint author.   II. Title.   III. Series.
Z8702.3.B57   [PN1998.A3]   016.79143'0233'0924   78–32027
ISBN 0–8161–7906–9

This publication is printed on permanent/durable acid-free paper
MANUFACTURED IN THE UNITED STATES OF AMERICA

Contents

Preface

Because Polanski's early short films were made in Poland, we had difficulty obtaining reliable information about them. The entries that follow, therefore, include only information confirmed in more than one source. His later screenplays also gave rise to some confusion with regard to the precise dates on which they were completed. In the case of produced screenplays, the release dates of the films are used; but, if the screenplays were unproduced, dates on which the actual writing was done are cited according to the best information available.

In the bibliography section, the languages covered are English, French, Polish and Czechoslovakian. For Czechoslovakian material, only references appearing in the *International Index to Film Periodicals* were consulted. In the case of Polish writings, the citations in the *International Index* are supplemented with materials obtained from the Polish Filmoteka Archives. French and English criticism was traced through additional indexes: *Reader's Guide, Film Literature Index, Alternative Press Index, The New Film Index, Chicorel's Index to Film Literature,* Mel Schuster's *Motion Picture Directors, The Critical Index* by Gerlach and Gerlach, *Art Index, Retrospective Index to Film Periodicals, Index to Critical Film Reviews* by Stephen Bowles, *British Humanities Index, Guide to the Performing Arts, International Index to Multi-Media Information, Media Review Digest, New York Times Index* and *New York Times Film Reviews Index, Popular Periodical Index, A Guide to Critical Reviews* by James Salem, *Variety* "Film Reviews Index" (Northwestern), Heinzkill's *Film Criticism: An Index to Critics' Anthologies,* specifically, in addition to general film reference guides.

References that we were unable to track down are indicated with an asterisk, and the source of the reference is noted in lieu of an annotation. In the case of the extensive bibliography in *Roman Polanski* by Jacques Belmans, the problem of tracing articles was particularly acute because a good number of the French publications listed there are not available in this country, and because Belmans's citations are often sketchy at best.

Many people generously assisted us in our efforts to compile data on Polanski. The critical survey section was formulated after fruitful discussions with Jerry Carlson; Patricia Erens and Julia Lesage gave advice on matters of style in other portions of the manuscript. Milos Stehlik and Zbigniew Koslowski provided translations for the Czech and Polish criticism, and Milos also helped us to obtain resource materials, as did Stuart Kaminsky. Translation for any Italian works consulted was done by Leah Maneaty, who, with William Lafferty, also translated some of the French material. Ruthann Schallert-Wygal typed the bulk of the manuscript, while Lilly Boruszkowksi also helped with research as well as with typing.

Margarita Snyder of Swank films was kind enough to arrange a special screening of *Macbeth,* and the American Film Institute gave permission to reprint the synopsis that appears in the AFI catalogue of Polanski's "River of Diamonds" ("Amsterdam") segment of *The Beautiful Swindlers.* Most valuable of all was the assistance of the Polish Filmoteka Archives, which gave us unique research materials. Without the contributions of all these people, our work would have been far more difficult and its results far less useful to others.

GB
VWW

September, 1978

Roman Polanski: Biography

Roman Polanski was born on August 18, 1933, of Polish-Jewish parents, in the Bastille section of Paris, where his father worked for the Tynan record company. When the boy was three, the family decided to move back to Poland, and, shortly thereafter, the Nazis invaded the country. In 1940, he watched the German troops build a wall across the end of the street on which he lived to seal off the Cracow ghetto. Though his father helped him to escape to the countryside, both of his parents were taken to concentration camps, and his mother later died at Auschwitz. The boy, meanwhile, boarded with a series of Catholic families in the country. They tried to instill their religion in him, but he had rejected it in favor of atheism by the time he was fourteen. Life in the country was difficult: Polanski recalls sleeping in barns where lice and fleas were his only companions. And, one day, while picking blackberries in a field, he was used for target practice by some passing German soldiers. Later, back in Cracow, the young boy was blown through a door by a German bomb after disobeying blackout regulations.

After the war, the boy's father returned to Cracow and remarried; however, Polanski chose to live alone. Hoping he would become an electrician, the elder Polanski enrolled his son in technical school, but the boy soon tired of this and, in 1950, transferred to art school. ("I was very bad in every subject except drawing,"[1] he says.) Meanwhile, he had become interested in acting and went to visit a local radio station that sponsored a children's program he was fond of. "I think the kids are very phony,"[2] he told the producers, referring to the child actors on the show. He was rewarded for his audacity by being given an opportunity to try out for a part himself. Soon, he was acting regularly for radio and did some theatrical work as well. Throughout his childhood, he supported himself by selling newspapers and doing odd jobs, using any extra cash to go to the movies. During the War, he saw German newsreels filled with anti-Jewish propaganda, and, later, American films dubbed into Polish. When he was sixteen, Polanski had another near brush with

1

death when an acquaintance from whom he was trying to buy a bicycle beat him over the head with a rock concealed in a newspaper.

In 1954, Polanski applied to the State Acting School, but was rejected on three different occasions in spite of his past acting experience, partly because his father ran a small plastics company, an activity frowned upon by the Communist regime as indicating too much private initiative. An additional drawback, Polanski later claimed, was that "some of the professors . . . thought I was too cocky."[3] Frustrated in his attempts to get into acting school, the young man tried for the comedians' school, but was again turned down. Desperate, and in imminent danger of being drafted, he went to Antoni Bohdziewicz, a professor at the State Film School at Lodz, who was also a theater director. Bohdziewicz suggested that he apply to the film directors' program. After taking a rigorous ten-day test, Polanski was accepted as one of six students. In the meantime, he had begun to act in the film productions of other students in the school and had played a role in Andrzej Wajda's *A Generation* (1954). In subsequent years, he continued to perform both in his own films and in those of others.

At the time Polanski entered, Lodz was generally considered to be the finest film school in the world, producing over the years such illustrious graduates as Wajda, Jerzy Skolimowski, and Kristof Zanussi. Also, during the 1950s there was an explosion of new ideas in the Polish cinema that emphasized a break with the past; this new activity was centered at the State Film School. The five-year directors' program at Lodz was a rigorous combination of liberal arts courses with intensive study of still photography, after which the students made their own films. While studying there, Polanski produced several short films, including *The Bike* (unfinished), *A Toothy Smile*, *The Lamp*, and *Break Up the Dance*, in which he staged an actual disruption of a school function using local delinquents and almost provoked the school authorities to dismiss him. During his fourth year, he made the prizewinning *Two Men and a Wardrobe* for extra credit. "It was the only film I've made that 'meant' something," he commented later. "It was about the intolerance of society toward somebody who is different."[4] He completed *When Angels Fall* in his fifth year as a diploma film.

In addition to the intensive formal program at Lodz, Polanski remembers his contacts with other students as a crucial part of his education. The school was housed in an old mansion, which had an imposing wooden staircase in the entry. There the students would engage in heated arguments about the merits of different schools of filmmaking. These experiences gave the young director firm aesthetic ideas about films. "There were schools of cinema within the school," he says. "My school was *Citizen Kane*, and the school of the older students . . . was *The Bicycle Thief*, and the postgraduates who were still hanging around were the Soviet-

Socialist Realism school—films like *Potemkin*."[5] When the students were not talking with one another or engaged in doing their own work, they were watching the films of others; as a result of the school's association with the Polish Film Archives, a wide variety of films from all parts of the world were screened continuously from eight in the morning to eight at night. The Polish directors whose work was studied included Munk, Bossak and Toeplitz.

After school, Polanski took a job as an assistant director with the Polish production company Kamera, where he worked with French documentary director J. M. Drot and assisted Andrzej Munk on *Bad Luck*. During 1960, Polanski also made another short on his own in Paris, *The Fat and the Lean*. He was briefly married at this time to Polish actress Barbara Kwiatkowska, but the couple was divorced in 1961. Polanski's final short film, *Mammals*, was made in Poland, and, according to a 1975 essay by Boleslaw Sulik, was financed privately by Voytek Frykowski. Frykowski, who also acts in the film, remained friends with the director until 1969, when he was murdered in Polanski's Bel Air home by members of the Charles Manson cult.

Polanski's next film, *Knife in the Water*, was feature-length. Shot in the Polish lakes region, the film was granted a small budget by the government, which Polanski exceeded—as he was to do on virtually every subsequent project. Though Warsaw officials halted the production midway through because of reports of orgies on the set, the movie was eventually completed. When it appeared in the Cannes and New York Film Festivals, it was widely praised, and it won an Academy Award Nomination for the best foreign film of 1964. Polanski went to New York for the film's American premiere and to Los Angeles for the Academy Awards ceremony, but was annoyed by the tendency of some critics to read Freudian symbolism into the film. In his own country, *Knife in the Water* was also enthusiastically received until Communist Party head Wladyslaw Gomulka denounced it for spreading corrupt Western attitudes, thus making it impossible for Polanski to obtain further funding for film projects in Poland.

Polanski settled again in Paris, where he soon discovered that his status as a celebrity could not easily be turned into financial backing to make new films. (He later compared his early experiences there with the life of the alienated Polish hero of *The Tenant*.) However, he was able to obtain some work in 1963 in Amsterdam directing a short segment titled "River of Diamonds" for the French compilation film *Les Plus Belles Escroqueries du Monde*. He also wrote a screenplay for French director Jean Leon called *Aimez-Vous Les Femmes?*, dealing with a group of Parisian cannibals who eat young girls for dinner.

Besides completing these small projects, Polanski established some useful associations while in France. Gerard Brach, a former publicist, worked as Polanski's co-author on the screenplays of the aforementioned films and collaborated with the director on most of his subsequent work. A fellow Pole, Gene Gutowski, arranged to finance the director's next film, *Repulsion*, in England in 1965. Polanski's and Brach's script for *Cul-de-Sac* had been finished before that of *Repulsion*, but it was only when the latter film became a success that money could be found to produce it. Before *Repulsion* began filming, Polanski and Brach had written still another screenplay which was never made. Titled *Cherchez La Femme*, it told of a divorced American dentist who looks for a wife in Europe after having grown dissatisfied with American women.

Though *Cul-de-Sac* is Polanski's own professed favorite among his films, it was not popular at the box office. Nonetheless, the London-based director was subsequently able to interest American producer Martin Ransohoff in another of his projects, *The Fearless Vampire Killers*. The film was initially to be the first of a three-picture contract the director entered into with Ransohoff. However, Ransohoff took Polanski's completed film and edited it for its American distribution, cutting twenty minutes, re-dubbing some of the voices, re-editing the music, and adding an animated prologue. Polanski has repeatedly denounced the Ransohoff version and has ascribed the movie's lack of commercial success in the United States to the producer's tampering. The two remaining pictures Polanski was to have done for Ransohoff were cancelled.

Polanski was shortly thereafter invited to Hollywood by producer William Castle to make the movie version of Ira Levin's best-selling novel *Rosemary's Baby*. After completing it in 1968, Polanski married actress Sharon Tate, who had starred in *The Fearless Vampire Killers*. The director has often referred to this time as the happiest of his life: *Rosemary's Baby* was both a critical and commercial success, and his wife was soon pregnant. He began work on several new projects. With Gene Gutowski, he produced *A Day at the Beach*, for which he had also written the screenplay; it was directed by Simon Hesera, a Moroccan, in Denmark. He also planned to direct two films himself. One, on violin virtuoso Nicholai Paganini, was being co-scripted by Ennio de Concini; another, called *Donner Pass*, dealt with cannibalism among American pioneers. On August 9, 1969, Polanski was at work on the screenplay of still another film, *Day of the Dolphin*, with Andrew Braunsberg and Michael Brown in London, when he received a call from his agent in Los Angeles telling him that his wife and three of his friends had been brutally murdered.

Polanski did not work as a director following this tragedy until 1971, when he made a film version of Shakespeare's *Macbeth* for Playboy productions. On this project, he was reunited with cameraman Gilbert Taylor, with whom he had had a falling-out after *Cul-de-Sac*. Polanski's disenchantment with the press for their handling of the Sharon Tate murders increased when he saw the *Macbeth* reviews, most of which objected to the amount of violence in the film. The following year Polanski wrote and directed *What?* for Italian producer Carlo Ponti, an episodic, sexually explicit Alice-In-Wonderland tale; it had little success with either critics or audiences.

After producing a documentary about his friend racing-car driver Jackie Stewart, Polanski returned to the United States to make *Chinatown*. Working on the script with Robert Towne in the home of producer Robert Evans "felt very uncomfortable," Polanski said later, "because the film is obviously written by someone who has got a great talent for the verbal side but none for the visual, and I was somehow constantly bored with the material."[6] The director changed the script's ending, substituting a more pessimistic one for Towne's original scene in which Evelyn Mulwray escapes from the police with Jake Gittes's help. On the set Polanski encountered more problems, this time with star Faye Dunaway and with cameraman Stanley Cortez, who was eventually re-placed with John Alonzo. But, in spite of these problems, *Chinatown* met with overwhelming critical and popular success on its release in the summer of 1974.

When *Chinatown* was released, Polanski had just completed a very different kind of project as the director of Berg's opera *Lulu* at the Spoleto festival in Italy. Though Robert Evans indicated at one point that he was planning to use Polanski on his next project, *Marathon Man*, that movie was ultimately directed by John Schlesinger. Another Polanski project, a swashbuckler that was to star Jack Nicholson, was also aban-doned. However, in 1976 he made *The Tenant* in Paris from a novel by Roland Topor, starring in the film as well as directing it. The critical reaction to his performance and to the film as a whole was largely unfavorable.

Following this setback, Polanski began work on other projects. One, called *The First Deadly Sin*, concerned a businessman obsessed with sexual perversion and homicide; another, *Hurricane*, was a remake of the John Ford film of the same name. But progress on these films was halted in mid-1977, when the director was arrested on charges of drug-ging and raping a 13-year-old girl at the home of his friend Jack Nicholson. After pleading guilty to having unlawful sexual intercourse with the girl, Polanski was given a ninety-day jail sentence for diagnostic purposes; however, the sentence was postponed so that he could work on *Hurricane*, from which he was subsequently dismissed by producer Dino de Laurentiis. After completing this period in prison, Polanski fled to France in order to avoid further criminal proceedings. In the summer of 1978, he worked in Paris on a film adaptation of Thomas Hardy's *Tess of the D'Urbervilles*.

Still boyish-looking at 44, the 5'4" Polanski's dedication to physical fitness has kept him in top physical condition. As a person, he is often described as charming, outgoing and argumentative. In addition to Polish and English, he speaks French, Russian and Italian fluently. Though he has little interest in politics, he does claim to be "more sympathetic to capitalism" than to communism, believing it to be "a stage to which people naturally evolved."[7] A firm believer in competition among men, he feels that women should let themselves be dominated. He disapproves of trade unions; in his mind they are "against nature."[3]

Most of his political stands are closely related to his work. Though he resigned from the Cannes Film Festival jury in 1968 out of sympathy for the French students' revolt, he objected strenuously when some of the New Wave directors revolted against the elitism of the festival itself. When *Rosemary's Baby* was condemned by the Catholic Legion of Decency and cut by the British censors, he spoke out in favor of freedom of expression; and he has often defended the violence in his films by arguing that it is only a reflection of the violence in life. Despite the problems that have continued to beset him in life, his work remains disciplined and accomplished. People who have worked with him speak with respect of his intimate knowledge of all phases of filmmaking and of his professional loyalty. Among the directors he admires are Federico Fellini, Stanley Kubrick, and Arthur Penn. He has said, "I always . . . wanted to be a film director, even before I really knew what it meant. Whatever I did in my life, I did towards that end."[9]

NOTES

1. Joseph Gelmis, "Roman Polanski," *The Film Director as Superstar* (Garden City, N.Y.: Doubleday, 1970), p. 142.
2. Gelmis, p. 142.
3. Larry DuBois, "Playboy Interview: Roman Polanski," *Playboy* (December, 1971), p. 116.
4. Gelmis, p. 145.
5. DuBois, p. 118.
6. American Film Institute, *Dialogue on Film: Roman Polanski*, 3, no. 8 (August, 1974), p. 2.
7. DuBois, p. 126.
8. Gelmis, p. 154.
9. Ivan Butler, *The Cinema of Roman Polanski*, The International Film Guide Series (New York: A. S. Barnes, 1970), p. 12.

Roman Polanski: Critical Survey

As a director who has been able to choose projects sympathetic to his interests when he has not actively developed screenplays on his own, Roman Polanski has produced a body of work that is markedly consistent both in subject matter and treatment. Known as a master of horror and the macabre, he has become identified with brilliantly executed depictions of sexuality and violence viewed with a coldly clinical eye. As an artist, Polanski is most commonly criticized for satisfying himself with technically accomplished renderings of sensational material without offering his audiences any moral perspective on it. Actually, his work does reveal a cohesive vision of the world, but it is a vision related more to individual psychology than to attitudes about a larger social or religious order. The director's relative lack of concern about these larger issues is not surprising given his early experiences. Growing up in Poland, he lived through both Nazi and Communist regimes, and, after having been born a Jew, he was raised as a Catholic. As one would expect, he seems to harbor a deeply cynical outlook about both politics and religion which is evident in his mature work whenever he treats these topics.

Polanski's early films show that this cynicism developed gradually. In his first widely distributed short, *Two Men and a Wardrobe*, made in 1958 when he was still in film school, the concern with social injustice is uppermost. In his next film, *When Angels Fall*, he explicitly attacked the sentimentalism about religion and the war fostered by the Polish Romantic tradition. In the film, an old peasant woman escapes from the distasteful realities of her present situation as an attendant in a public toilet by indulging in fantasies about her life that are inspired by images from popular Polish genre paintings. Events from her past— including the First World War—are sentimentalized in this way, as is her vision of her future in heaven. Polanski's first feature film, *Knife in the Water* (1962), is also something of an anomaly compared to the director's later efforts in its concern with material success as a method of achieving social status (though this element in the film has been attributed to Polanski's co-writer Jerzy Skolimowski).

In most of Polanski's later work, these conventional social and religious touchstones are superseded by an aesthetically-based involvement with elements taken from the Theater of the Absurd and Surrealism, his two major artistic influences. The Absurdist conviction that man is isolated in a meaningless decaying universe finds expression in Polanski's films, and he also shows an Absurdist's interest in burlesque and parody. Like the Surrealists, he enjoys exploring deviant behavior, often of a sexual nature: incest, cannibalism, suicide, homosexuality, transvestitism, and homicidal mania are subjects he returns to again and again. Another device that Polanski borrows from the Surrealists is the distortion of reality through bizarre, unexpected details.

Though both of these influences are evident in everything Polanski has done, in his later films one or the other dominates. The Absurdist outlook is most evident in his movies about tensions existing within groups of people, rather than within a single individual. These are his least naturalistic films but the most comic ones, using simple character types often based on literary rather than realistic models. A few are almost totally immersed in parody and they are the lightest in mood: *The Fearless Vampire Killers* (a spoof of vampire myths) and *What?* (based on *Alice in Wonderland*). Here the spirit of innocent fantasy is supported by bright colors and picturesque compositions. In his blacker Absurdist comedies, however, Polanski's compositions revert to their characteristic starkness which, combined with his use of deep-focus photography, emphasizes the distance between his characters in films like *Knife in the Water*, *Cul-De-Sac*, *Mammals*, and *The Fat and the Lean*. All of the Absurdist films focus on shifting power relationships, usually precipitated by the arrival of an outsider into a group, which forces a reshuffling of status and privilege. Polanski eliminates society by locating the action in isolated settings: a boat on a deserted lake in *Knife in the Water*, a castle in *Fearless Vampire Killers* and *Cul-De-Sac*, a villa on the Italian Riviera in *What?*, a vast, snow-covered field in *Mammals*. Settings such as these stress the characters' isolation from the world around them as well as from one another; and the director's preference for musical accompaniments of cool-sounding jazz or tunelessly atonal rhythms (often by Krzysztof Komeda) reinforces the sense of desolation.

Similar music sets an even bleaker mood in Polanski's horror films. These focus on individuals rather than groups, and, in their emphasis on blending elements from the external world with projections from the inner landscape of their protagonists, they draw heavily on the tradition of Surrealism. Movies like *Repulsion*, *Rosemary's Baby*, and *The Tenant* terrify audiences because, to some extent, they force us to share the confusions of their main characters about the difference between social persecution and paranoid delusion. In *Rosemary's Baby*, the persecution is discovered to be genuine, while in *Repulsion* and *The Tenant* it is only imagined. But, in each case, the effect depends on the audience sharing the fears and uncertainties of the hero or heroine through surrealistic devices such as dreams and hallucinations. A sense of strangeness in the everyday is communicated by exaggerated sound effects such as dripping faucets or by close-ups of odd visual details such as sprouting potatoes.

Like the Absurdist comedies, these films isolate their characters from the surrounding world. But here the protagonists are restricted to their apartments, which, with their long halls and barricaded doorways, suggest Freudian overtones. At times, Polanski emphasizes the subjective nature of these dwellings through wide-angle lens distortion, which makes the spaces appear either cavernous or claustrophobically womb-like. The violation of the apartment is explicitly connected with the violation of the protagonist's own body in *The Tenant*, in which Trelkovsky's anxiety about his right to occupy Simone Choule's quarters is echoed in his confusion about the nature of his own physical identity, and in *Rosemary's Baby*, in which Rosemary's fear for the child inside her finds external expression in her desire to make her new apartment her own and to keep it safe and separate from the sinister activities in the apartment of her neighbors. This concern with the contamination of one's physical identity finds an outlet not only in Polanski's expressionistic rendering of the setting, but also in his references to unpalatable food: the garbage in *The Tenant*, a putrefying skinned rabbit in *Repulsion*, a suspiciously "chalky" chocolate mousse in *Rosemary's Baby*. Details such as these cause Polanski's protagonists to feel physically endangered even when locked in their own apartments.

It is not only the physical environment that threatens the protagonists in Polanski's horror films, it is the social one as well. Unlike the characters in the Absurdist films who are cut off from the surrounding world, these individuals are faced by a society that is continually intruding on them, promoting a sexual disgust that makes a mature sexual relationship impossible to sustain. Wrinkled old people are invariably prominent and are often shown nude or in other unflattering ways. Other members of society, such as Trelkovsky's office mates and the pub-crawlers in *Repulsion*, are overly familiar and crass, prompting an equally strong feeling of distaste. Even objects belonging to others can arouse revulsion: a tannis root pendant in *Rosemary's Baby*, a toothbrush in *Repulsion*. The unsavory portrait of society in these films makes it seem inevitable that the hero or heroine's attempts at establishing a nurturing love relationship will end in failure: Rosemary in *Rosemary's Baby* becomes increasingly alienated from her husband after dreaming that he has turned into the devil; Carol in *Repulsion* cannot bear to have her boyfriend kiss her any more than he can bear it when a male friend jokingly kisses him in the pub; Trelkovsky in *The Tenant* is unable to consummate his affair with the good-natured Stella after having been the recipient of similar familiarities from an overweight co-worker at his housewarming party. Rosemary and Carol also try to establish other, non-sexual ties, but these too are denied them and, like Trelkovsky, they finally find themselves alone in a hostile universe.

Many of the techniques used in the horror films to communicate a sense of solitude in a threatening world are repeated in Polanski's more Absurdist work. But here there is less interest in the psychological etiology of the threat than in the black-comic interplay between characters who are either callous exploiters or willing victims. Caught in an irrational universe, they are unable to locate meaningful values with which to order their lives and are reduced to spending their time in pointless squabbling. In *Knife in the Water*, the issue of murder is seen only in terms of its value to the wife in the power game she is playing with her husband. In *What?*, Nancy's naive desire to learn something of value from the inhabitants of the villa seems ludicrous in the context of their base preoccupations. And, in *Cul-De-Sac*, the gangster Richard continues to call his employer Katelbach, but Katelbach refuses to help him escape from the petty concerns of George and Teresa, even though his partner Albie is dying.

This vision of an uncaring, meaningless universe accounts for the overwhelmingly pessimistic tone of Polanski's films, in which consistently circular plots leave the characters no better off at the end than they were at the beginning. Most often, in fact, Polanski's heroes are much worse off as a result of what happens to them, and the director shows this in characteristically psychological terms by including imagery that suggests regression. Rosemary Woodhouse and Carol Ledoux look increasingly childlike as their problems multiply, both because of their little-girl attire and, in Rosemary's case, because of her haircut. Nancy, in *What?*, suffers an even worse fate by losing her clothes altogether, and being forced at one point to cover herself with a napkin arranged as a bib. In *The Tenant*, Trelkovsky helplessly allows Stella to undress him and, in *Cul-De-Sac*, George submits to being garishly dressed up in a woman's nightgown by Teresa. This motif of regression, which recurs in almost all of the films, reflects a steady ebbing away of the self in a world that offers no solid moorings on which to build a mature identity. In such a world, people are forced to retreat back to earlier behavior patterns, though these, too, ultimately prove useless, making the individual feel even more powerless and easily threatened.

Regression's terrors and temptations are most pervasively expressed through Polanski's water imagery. The psychoanalytical implications of this motif are obvious at the end of *Cul-De-Sac*, when George is pictured in a fetal position atop a rock in the middle of a flooded causeway, plaintively calling out the name of his former wife. But, for Polanski, the meaning of water goes beyond Freudianism; his films connect regression with an amoral universe. In *Knife in the Water*, the very title suggests the futility of human progress in a world without anchors. "Floating on water is nothing. It's nothing," the youth comments at one point in the film (which takes place almost entirely aboard a small boat). "Only when you have to move ahead on foot, a knife is necessary." This inability to move ahead is common to all of Polanski's heroes. Frustrated in their attempts to integrate mature personalities by the absence of ethical touchstones in the world around them, they are gradually reduced to floundering helplessly in a morass of chaotic violence and finally to a state of helpless stasis.

This pattern repeats itself in two Polanski projects initially conceived by others: *Macbeth* and *Chinatown*. Both resemble the horror films in that they focus on a single protagonist trapped in a threatening world. But in these films the theme is integrated with overtly political material supplied by Shakespeare and screenwriter Robert Towne. Polanski uses this new dimension to enlarge on his view that the world offers nothing to guide the individual to meaningful action. *Macbeth* illustrates this by stressing senseless brutality from the outset; and the predominantly grey, rainy weather paints the violence in despairing tones. Ross's new role as an unscrupulous political opportunist who survives all the political purges unscathed shows the society as one that rewards such qualities, while Donalbain's final meeting with the same witches who corrupted Macbeth suggests an endless cycle of political Machiavellianism. Not surprisingly, Polanski's protagonist seems hopelessly unequal to this ruthless world. In the final battle, he is alone, and his cumbersome armor even denies him the heroic stature that would result from going to a glorious death.

In *Chinatown*, the hero is similarly ill-equipped to do battle with a degenerate society. But here Polanski enlarges on the political dimension of the screenplay by explicitly connecting the corruption with his theme of regression—though in this case he focuses on regression in an evolutionary, rather than a psychological, sense. In the film, Jake Gittes himself does return to a former state, but our fears for him arise more from the chaos we feel in the physical environment than from the kind of expressions of regressive behavior we see in other Polanski protagonists. Especially disturbing is the breakdown of expected distinctions between water and land, which continually poses the threat of drowning. Noah Cross's remark about tidepools as "the place where life begins" is echoed in a negative way by the fish imagery attached to politically powerful people like Cross, who trample on the most fundamental rules of society with primeval disregard for civilized values.

In *Chinatown* and *Macbeth*, Polanski's vision encompasses areas he does not ordinarily concern himself with, and, for this reason, these films allow a fuller definition of his themes. Together with his other projects, they reveal an artist who presents infantile expressions of violence and sexuality as the highest forms of activity to which human beings can aspire in a universe without values. In a world like this, the impossibility of constructive human contact makes regression inevitable. For the most part, Polanski views this state of affairs coldly, refusing to permit audiences to feel for his characters what the characters are unable to feel for one another. Yet, at times, he pictures what has been lost with a touching poignancy: George on a rock wailing for his wife at the end of *Cul-De-Sac*, Jake Gittes staring at Evelyn Mulwray's daughter on the stairs in *Chinatown*. At such moments the director provides us not simply with a sardonic understanding of what is, but with a painful awareness of what might have been. This awareness saves Polanski's films from total nihilism, for it suggests that human isolation is not inevitable, that compassion, however fleeting, can exist.

VIRGINIA WRIGHT WEXMAN

September, 1978

The Films:
Synopses, Credits and Notes, Major Awards

[*Items preceded by an asterisk (*) have not been seen by the compilers.]

*1 THE BICYCLE [Rower] (1955)

Synopsis

Early short film made at the National Film School of Poland (unfinished), unavailable for screening.

Credits and Notes

Unfinished; credit information not available.

*2 A TOOTHY SMILE (1957)

Synopsis

Early short film made at the National Film School of Poland, unavailable for screening.

Credits and Notes

Credit information not available.

*3 BREAK UP THE DANCE [Rozbijemy Zabawe] (1957)

Synopsis

Early short film made at the National Film School of Poland, unavailable for screening.

Credits and Notes

Director:	Roman Polanski
Screenplay:	Roman Polanski
Photography:	Andrzej Galinski

*4 THE CRIME [Morderstwo] (1957)

Synopsis

Early short film made at the National Film School of Poland, unavailable for screening.

Credits and Notes

Credit information not available.

5 TWO MEN AND A WARDROBE [Dwaj Ludzie Z Szasa] (1958)

Synopsis

Two men carrying an old-fashioned wardrobe with a mirror on the front emerge from the sea. When they reach the beach, they shake the water off themselves and do a little dance together. Then they take the wardrobe into a city. There they try to get on a crowded streetcar but are pushed off by some youths who are standing in the doorway. Carrying their burden to a deserted street, the men are delighted to notice a pretty girl. At first she seems friendly, but, when she sees the wardrobe, she turns and walks away. The two men continue their wanderings with the wardrobe, taking it along an embankment by a river. Two homosexuals watch them from a bridge and giggle, but all the while one is stealing the other's wallet. A restaurant proprietor is the next person to turn away the two men with their wardrobe. Shortly afterward, they are also rejected by the concierge of a small hotel, though he enthusiastically welcomes a group of women with suitcases who arrive as the men depart.

Nearby, a gang of boys throw rocks at a kitten. Noticing an attractive young woman, they try to stalk her. But the woman sees them in the mirror of the wardrobe as the two comrades pass by, and walks off. Enraged, the gang members turn on the men with the wardrobe and beat them. Afterward, the two dress each other's wounds by the river as a drunk lingers in the vicinity. Then they rest in a junkyard filled with old barrels. The watchman, however, soon discovers them and they are beaten again. The two men then turn into the woods where, beside a stream, one man is beating another's head in with a rock. Finally the men with the wardrobe reach the beach again. There they find a little boy making scores of identical sand castles. Picking their way among these, the comrades retreat with their wardrobe back into the sea.

Credits and Notes

Director:	Roman Polanski
Screenplay:	Roman Polanski
Photography:	Maciej Kijowski
Music:	Kryzsztof Komeda-Trzcinski
Cast:	Henryk Kluba, Jakub Goldberg, Roman Polanski.
Production:	Polish Film Academy, Lodz
Distribution:	Contemporary
Running Time:	15 minutes

Major Awards

"Golden Gates" Award for Best Experimental Film at International Film Festival, San Francisco, 1958

Third Place Award for Experimental Film at International Exhibition of Experimental Films, Brussels, 1958

Honorable Mention, International Short Film Festival, Oberhausen, 1959

*6 THE LAMP [*Lampa*] (1959)

Synopsis

Early short film made at the National Film School of Poland, unavailable for screening.

Credits and Notes

Director:	Roman Polanski
Screenplay:	Roman Polanski
Photography:	A. Krzysztof
Production:	Polish Film Academy, Lodz

7 WHEN ANGELS FALL [*Gdy Spadaja Anioly*] (1959)

Synopsis

Early in the morning, an old woman goes along a deserted street to her job as custodian of a public men's room. As she sits facing the urinals, all kinds of men come and go, and, as she watches them, various sounds and images trigger a series of picturesque fantasies about her youth. She recalls that as a young girl she had a romance with a soldier, who left her pregnant. She neglected her duties on her father's farm to care for her baby and watched over the child tenderly as it grew up.

The sight of a police officer arresting a drunk in the men's room disrupts her reverie, but she eventually indulges in more fantasies about her youth. Her son was taken away to the army. She followed the boy to the town where his regiment was stationed, but he rejected the parcel she tried to give him. The boy eventually went into battle, where he saw a companion's legs shot off and killed an enemy soldier who wanted to make friends with him. Later, he was killed himself.

As night falls, the old woman's fantasies fade, and she finds herself alone in the men's room. But the silence is interrupted by the sound of the skylight breaking, and she imagines that her son has returned as an angel to claim her.

Credits and Notes

Director:	Roman Polanski
Screenplay:	Roman Polanski
Photography:	Henryk Kucharski
Music:	Krzysztof Komeda-Trzcinski
Cast:	Barbara Kwiatkowska, Jakub Goldberg, Roman Polanski, Henryk Kluba.

Roman Polanski plays role of an old woman; made for film school diploma.

8 THE FAT AND THE LEAN [Le Gros et Le Maigre] (1961)

Synopsis

On a scruffy lawn outside of an unkempt house, a fat man sits in a rocking chair, ordering a small, thin servant about. The servant eagerly performs various tasks in order to please his master: feeding him, carrying his bedpan, playing the flute for his amusement. He even dances to the rhythm of a drum beaten by the fat man.

Tempted by the lure of the city, which is visible in the distance, the thin man decides to leave. But, when his master presents him with a goat, he changes his mind, though the fact that the goat is chained to his leg restricts his freedom even further. Eventually, the fat man unchains the goat, for which act of generosity his servant is so grateful that he becomes more obsequious than ever before.

NOTE: It has been at least five years since the compilers last viewed *The Fat and the Lean*. The preceding plot summary has been pieced together from memory and some notes; to verify details, other synopses of the film were consulted.

Credits and Notes

Director:	Roman Polanski
Screenplay:	Roman Polanski, Jean-Pierre Rousseau
Photography:	Jean-Michel Boussaguet
Editor:	Roman Polanski
Music	Krzysztof Komeda-Trzcinski
Cast:	Roman Polanski, Andre Katelbach.
Production:	Claude Joudioux/A.P.E.C. (Paris)
Running Time:	16 minutes

9 KNIFE IN THE WATER [Nóż W Wodzie] (1962)

Synopsis

Andrzej, a successful sports journalist, and Krystyna, his wife, are driving their Mercedes-Benz to take a brief holiday aboard their sailboat. En route, they are summarily stopped by a young hitchhiker who has planted himself in the middle of the road. Andrzej, who is driving, gives the youth a lift as far as the harbor. As they drive, the youth admires the luxury of the journalist's car. At the harbor, the couple load their boat with the boy's help; he is just about to leave when Andrzej calls him back and invites him to accompany them on their trip, saying, "Want to go on with the game?" The boy accepts.

During breakfast on the boat, the youth takes out a knife and demonstrates a game in which he stabs the weapon rapidly between the fingers of his outstretched hand. After eating, he helps Andrzej man the boat as Krystyna sunbathes. After towing the boat through some reeds, a particularly arduous task, the youth wants to leave, but is dissuaded by Andrzej. At lunch, the young man mocks Andrzej for carrying a hot container of soup with a hand-grip; but, when the boy tries to grasp it with his bare hands, he burns his palms—though he suffers the pain in silence. Finally, Krystyna pulls his hands apart, spilling the soup in the process. The boy again begins to talk of leaving. When he is told that the boat cannot move because there is no wind, he tries to row. Goaded by the couple's laughter at his ineffectual attempts to get to the shore, he throws the oar he has been using into the water. Krystyna swims out to retrieve it, then begins to play in the water with an inflatable crocodile as Andrzej and the boy play with the knife. Then Andrzej joins his wife in the water. Unexpectedly, the wind rises, and the boy is unable to control the craft. Eventually, however, he manages to maneuver it so that Krystyna and Andrzej are able to climb back on board. Later, as the boat threatens to run aground in the shallows, Andrzej is forced to use the youth's knife to cut the halyard. When it begins to rain, the boat is anchored and the three go below. There the two men engage in a contest to see which can blow up his air mattress faster. Even though Andrzej is using a mechanical pump, the boy wins. Then they all begin a game of pick-up-sticks. When Krystyna makes an error, the youth asks her to sing a song to pay her forfeit as Andrzej listens to a boxing match on the radio with earphones. Then Krystyna asks the boy to recite a poem. Afterward all three retire for the night.

Early the next morning, the youth joins Krystyna on deck. Andrzej appears and begins to order the youth about in an effort to get the boat in motion again. When he discovers that the journalist has taken possession of his knife, the boy tries to reclaim it, but Andrzej, intending to embed the weapon in the mast, throws it instead into the water. The two men struggle, and the youth is eventually thrown into the lake. Fearing that the young man has drowned, the couple searches for him, but fail to see him hiding behind a buoy. Prodded by his wife's accusations that he is a murderer, Andrzej swims for shore to inform the police about the youth's death. Meanwhile, the boy comes back on board the boat and makes love to Krystyna. Dropping her passenger off before she reaches the harbor where Andrzej is waiting for her, Krystyna at first says nothing to her husband about the boy's return. But, as they drive back, she confesses the whole truth. Andrzej stops the car at a fork in the road that will take him either toward the police station or toward home, unable to choose between confessing that he has accidentally caused the boy's death or believing that his wife has been unfaithful to him.

Credits and Notes

Producer:	Stanislaw Zylewicz
Director:	Roman Polanski
Screenplay:	Jerzy Skolimowski, Jakub Goldberg, Roman Polanski
Photography:	Jerzy Lipman
Camera:	Andrzej Kostenko
Editor:	Halina Prugar
Music:	Krzysztof Komeda-Trzcinski

Sound:	Halina Paszkowska
Cast:	Leon Niemczyk (Andrzej), Jolanta Umecka (Krystyna), Zygmunt Malanawicz (Youth).
Production:	Kamera Film Unit for Film Polski

Released in Poland in 1962.

Distribution:	Kanawha Films
Running Time:	94 minutes
Released:	October 28, 1963
Alternate Titles:	*The Young Lover, The Long Sunday*

Major Awards

First Prize at International Film Festival, Venice, 1962
International Film Critics' Award at International Film Festival, Venice, 1962
"Cinema 60" Award at International Film Festival, Venice, 1962
Grand Prix at Film Gatherings, Prades, 1963
Academy Awards Nomination as Best Foreign Film, 1963

10 MAMMALS [*Ssaki*] (1962)

Synopsis

One man pulls another in a sleigh over a vast field of snow while the man in the sleigh plucks a chicken. Soon, however, the man who is pulling tires of his task and pushes his companion off the sleigh so that he can ride himself. Taking out his knitting, he prepares to enjoy his ride, but his ball of wool rolls off the sleigh almost immediately. While he is retrieving it, the other man obviously pulls the sleigh along, and, as soon as the man with the knitting catches up and climbs on for his ride, he is ordered off again. When he protests, the man with the chicken pretends that he has a nosebleed. His friend then agrees to pull, but soon feigns a stomach ache. This game proceeds at an ever-increasing pace until the two both wrap themselves in bandages simultaneously and begin to fight. At this point, the sleigh is appropriated by a third man who is camped nearby. When the two comrades stop fighting, they cannot find the sleigh anywhere. Resignedly, they exchange the chicken and the knitting and stroll off arm-in-arm. But soon one pretends to have a nosebleed again and asks his friend to carry him on his back. In this way, they begin their game anew and continue changing positions as they disappear into the distance.

Credits and Notes

Director:	Roman Polanski
Screenplay:	A. Kondraciuk, Roman Polanski
Photography:	Andrzej Kostenko
Music:	Krzysztof Komeda-Trzcinski
Editors:	Halina Prugar, J. Niedzwiedzka
Cast:	Henryk Kluba, Michal Zolnierkiewicz.
Production:	Studio Se-Ma-For, Lodz

Filmed before *Knife in the Water*; however, edited afterward.

Distribution:	Connoisseur
Running Time:	11 minutes

Major Awards

Grand Prix at International Short Film Festival, Tours, 1963
Award at International Short Film Festival, Oberhausen, 1963

°11 **THE BEAUTIFUL SWINDLERS** [*Les Plus Belles Escroqueries Du Monde*] (1963)

Synopsis

"AMSTERDAM: A young Parisian woman in Amsterdam cons a middle-aged Dutchman into buying her a diamond necklace, presumably with the promise that she will in return give him certain 'favors.' She flees from his house with the expensive jewelry, however, before fulfilling her end of the bargain. But her motives are entirely unmercenary: she trades her acquisition for a parrot being sold by a waterfront bum who is unaware of the necklace's value."

[Reprinted from American Film Institute, *The American Film Institute Catalog of Motion Pictures Produced in the United States, Feature Films, 1961–1970* (New York: R. R. Bowker Company, 1976), p. 72, by permission of The American Film Institute. Copyright 1976 by The American Film Institute.]

Credits and Notes

Episode: "A River of Diamonds"

Producer:	Pierre Roustang
Director:	Roman Polanski
Screenplay:	Roman Polanski, Gerard Brach
Photography:	Jerzy Lipman
Editor:	Rita Von Royen
Music:	Krzysztof Komeda-Trzcinski
English Subtitles:	Herman G. Weinberg
Cast:	Nicole Karen, Jan Teulings, Arnold Gelderman.
Production:	Ulysse Productions, Primex Films, Lux Films, Vides, Toho Company, Caesar Films

Filmed in Amsterdam. Episode also included with two other short films in film *Cinema Different Three* (1970). Opened in Paris in August, 1964; scheduled for distribution in the United States originally as *World's Greatest Swindles.*

Distribution:	Ellis Films, Continental Distributing, Incorporated
Running Time:	90 minutes
Released:	September 12, 1967
Original Title:	"Amsterdam"

12 REPULSION (1965)

Synopsis

Carol Ledoux, a manicurist, lives with her sister Helen and works in a London beauty shop run by Madame Denise. One day during her lunch hour, Carol encounters Colin, who has been courting her. Colin asks her to dinner that evening, but she refuses, explaining that she is eating with her sister. Colin then makes a dinner date with her for the following evening. Later, after Carol arrives home, Helen's boyfriend Michael arrives, and the couple decide to go out to dinner, leaving Carol alone. Carol goes to bed, but is awakened by the sounds of love-making in the next room. In the morning, she unexpectedly surprises Michael shaving in the bathroom.

At the beauty shop, Carol listens to the love problems of Bridget, a fellow employee. As she walks along the street after work, Carol is stopped by Colin, who is annoyed that she has forgotten their dinner date. Colin drives her home, but she seems preoccupied and is unresponsive to his attempts to kiss her. Later, in her room, she cries because her sister is going away on a trip with Michael. The next day at work Carol seems so preoccupied that Madame Denise assumes she must be ill and sends her home in a taxi. Alone in the apartment, Carol begins to hallucinate, imagining that there is a strange man attacking her and that cracks are opening up in the wall. For the next three days, she does not go to her job, and the apartment is shown in an increasing state of disarray.

When Carol does return to the beauty shop, she stabs the finger of one of the customers with the manicure scissors and is summarily dismissed by Madame Denise. Back at home alone, Carol is upset by the arrival of Colin, who is worried about her in spite of the efforts of his friends, Reggie and John, to discourage his interest in the young manicurist. Colin breaks down the door to get in and, as he tries to tell her about his feelings, Carol bludgeons him to death with a heavy candlestick. Then she barricades the front door and puts Colin's body in a bathtub full of water. After several more days have passed, the landlord breaks into the apartment to collect the rent. But Carol murders him also by repeatedly slashing him with Michael's razor. At last, Helen and Michael return from their trip and are horrified to find the apartment in chaos and Carol lying under her bed in a state of catatonia.

Credits and Notes

Presentation:	Michael Klinger, Tony Tenser
Producer:	Gene Gutowski
Director:	Roman Polanski
Screenplay:	Roman Polanski, Gerard Brach
Photography:	Gilbert Taylor
Camera Operator:	Alan Hall
Art Director:	Seamus Flannery
Assistant Art Director:	Frank Willson
Production Controller:	Terry Glinwood
Music:	Chico Hamilton
Orchestration:	Gabor Szabo
Sound Editor:	Tom Priestly

Sound Mixer: Leslie Hammond
Sound Supervisor: Stephen Dalby
Sound Recordist: Gerry Humphreys
Editor: Alastair McIntyre
Assistant Editor: Karen Howard
First Assistant
   Director: Ted Sturgis
Make-Up: Tom Smith
Hairdresser: Gladys Leakey
Adaptation and addi-
   tional dialogue: David Stone
Continuity: Dee Vaughan
Still Photographer: Laurie Turner
Props: Alf Pegley
Associate Producers: Robert Sterne, Sam Waynberg
Cast: Catherine Deneuve (Carol), Ian Hendry (Michael), John Fraser (Colin), Yvonne Furneaux (Helen), Patrick Wymark (Landlord), Renee Houston (Miss Balch), Valerie Taylor (Madame Denise), James Villiers (John), Helen Fraser (Bridget), Hugh Futcher (Reggie), Mike Pratt (Workman), Monica Merlin (Mrs. Rendlesham), Imogen Graham (Manicurist).
Production: Compton/Tekli Film Productions

Filmed on location in London. Opened in London in June, 1965.

Distribution: Royal Films International
Running Time: 104 minutes
Released: October 3, 1965

Major Awards

Silver Bear Award at Film Festival, Berlin, 1965

13 CUL-DE-SAC (1966)

Synopsis

Two gangsters, Albert and Richard, find themselves stranded on a causeway when their car breaks down on a remote part of the English coast. While Richard, who has been shot in the arm, goes to get help, the critically wounded Albert remains in the car, which gradually becomes inundated with water as the tide rises over the causeway. Meanwhile, Richard discovers a castle inhabited by George, a retired businessman, and his beautiful young second wife, Teresa. George passes the time by painting portraits of Teresa, while Teresa amuses herself by carrying on a playful affair with Christopher, their neighbors' son.

Richard hides in the chicken house next to the castle and falls asleep as George and Teresa prepare to eat dinner. Annoyed that Teresa has brought back only five shrimp from a shrimping expedition she has been on with Christopher, George finally decides to cook himself a boiled egg as Teresa sits on the floor painting her toenails. Later, as Teresa teases George by dressing him up in her nightgown and makeup, Richard breaks into the castle. When the couple discovers him, the gangster brandishes a gun and takes them prisoner. Richard anxiously telephones his employer, Mr. Katelbach, to come and rescue his partner and himself; but Mr. Katelbach, dissatisfied with the way in which Richard and Albert have bungled their last assignment, never appears. Richard forces George and Teresa to go back with him to the car and push it to the castle, where Albert soon dies from his wounds. After locking George and Teresa in their bedroom, Richard spends the night digging a grave for his friend. Eventually Teresa, who has escaped from the bedroom through a window, helps him in his task. In the morning, when the grave is almost ready, the two let George out of the bedroom and force him to go down into it to finish the digging, throwing the corpse on top of him.

The day brings guests: Cecil and Jacqueline, a vacuous, fashion-minded couple, and Philip and Marion Fairweather, who bring along their undisciplined son Horace. For the duration of their visit, Richard unwillingly plays the role of a servant. George grows increasingly irritated by his guests, especially Horace, and, when the boy breaks a window while playing with a gun, he demands that they all leave. George and Teresa are then left alone once more with Richard. Goaded into action by his wife, George finally shoots and kills their captor, after which he goes berserk. An alarmed Teresa escapes with Cecil, who has returned to claim his rifle, and George is left alone, still raving. We last see him sitting on a rock near the highway calling out the name of his first wife as the tide comes in around him.

Credits and Notes

Producer:	Gene Gutowski
Director:	Roman Polanski
Screenplay:	Roman Polanski, Gerard Brach
Translation:	John Sutro
Photography:	Gilbert Taylor B.S.C.
Camera Operators:	Geoffrey Seaholme, Roy Ford
Special Effects:	Bowie Films Ltd.
Art Director:	George Lack
Production Designer:	Voytek
Music:	Krzysztof Komeda-Trzcinski
Sound Supervisor:	Stephen Dalby
Sound Editor:	David Campling
Sound Mixer:	George Stephenson
Costumes:	Bridget Sellers
Editor:	Alastair McIntyre
First Assistant Directors:	Ted Sturgis, Roger Simons
Make-Up:	Alan Brownie
Hairdresser:	Joyce James
Continuity:	Dee Vaughan
Still Photographer:	Laurie Turner
Props:	Alf Pegley

Casting:	Maude Spector
Production Manager:	Don Weeks
Production Con- troller:	Terry Glinwood
Production Super- visor:	Robert Sterne
Executive Producer:	Sam Waynberg
Cast:	Donald Pleasance (George), Francoise Dorleac (Teresa), Lionel Stander (Richard), Jack MacGowran (Albert), Iain Quarrier (Christopher), Geoffrey Sumner (Christopher's Father), Renee Houston (Christopher's Mother), Robert Dorning (Philip Fairweather), William Franklyn (Cecil), Jacqueline Bisset (Jacqueline), Trevor Delaney (Horace).
Production:	Compton/Tekli Film Productions

Filmed on location at Holy Island, Northumberland.
Opened in London in June, 1966; running time 111 minutes.

Distribution:	Sigma III Corporation
Running Time:	107 minutes
Released:	November 7, 1966

Major Awards

Golden Bear Award at Film Festival, Berlin, 1966

14   THE FEARLESS VAMPIRE KILLERS OR PARDON ME, BUT YOUR TEETH ARE IN MY NECK (1967)

Synopsis

Professor Abronsius and his assistant Alfred travel by sleigh to a remote part of Transylvania in order to investigate rumors of vampires in the area. Arriving at an inn, they discover garlic hung on the rafters and are impressed by the fearful attitude of the innkeeper, Shagal. They conclude that a vampire's castle must be nearby.

Captivated by Shagal's lovely daughter Sarah, Alfred is appalled when he witnesses her being carried off from her bath by the vampire Count Von Krolock. While searching for his missing daughter, Shagal is bitten by the vampires. He, in turn, bites the maid Magda, whose cross does not deter him because he is Jewish. Alfred and Abronsius pursue Shagal to the castle where the Count's hunchbacked servant, Koukol, takes them to see his master. The Count and the professor enjoy a conversation about the latter's work on bats, after which Koukol escorts Abronsius and Alfred to bedrooms where they will spend the night. On the way, they encounter Herbert, the Count's son, who shows a pronounced interest in Alfred.

The next day, Alfred and the professor set out to locate the crypt in which the vampires sleep. When they find it, however, Abronsius is unable to squeeze through the narrow window into the room. His assistant, who has slipped through before him, tries to pull the professor through, but he remains wedged in the window opening. Alfred, therefore, is charged with the task of destroying the vampires, but he is too terrified to drive the spikes into their hearts. On his way back outside to extricate his master from the window, Alfred comes upon Sarah bathing. However, after telling him that there is to be a ball that evening, she disappears. Alfred then rescues the professor. However, when he returns to find Sarah again, he comes instead upon Herbert who, with his father, chases Alfred and Abronsius around the castle. Finally, the two would-be vampire killers are locked up together in one of the tower rooms. By lighting an ancient cannon on the room's balcony, however, they manage to blow a hole through the door and escape. Then, disguised in appropriate period costumes that they find in the castle, the professor and his assistant join the vampires' ball below. Once there, they encounter Sarah and convince her to flee with them. Their escape is abruptly precipitated when the other partygoers notice that the images of Abronsius and Alfred are reflected in the ballroom mirror, proving that they are not vampires. Pursued by the Count and his guests, the three are nonetheless able to make their way to a sleigh and drive off into the night. But, as they leave the castle, Sarah, who has already been infected by the vampires, sinks her teeth into the slumbering Alfred's neck as the unknowing Abronsius drives unconcernedly on.

Credits and Notes

Producer:	Gene Gutowski
Director:	Roman Polanski
Screenplay:	Gerard Brach, Roman Polanski
Translation of Original French Script:	Gillian Sutro, John Sutro
Photography:	Douglas Slocombe
Camera Operator:	Chic Waterson
Title Design:	Andre Francois
Art Director:	Fred Carter
Production Designer:	Wilfred Shingleton
Music:	Christopher Komeda [Krzsztof Komeda-Trzcinski]
Sound Editor:	Lionel Selwyn
Sound Recording:	George Stephenson
Dubbing Mixer:	Len Shilton
Costumes:	Sophie Devine
Choreography:	Tutte Lemkow
Editor:	Alastair McIntyre
Assistant Director:	Roy Stevens
Makeup:	Tom Smith
Hairdresser:	Biddy Chrystal
Continuity:	Helen Whitson
Production Manager:	David W. Orton
Executive Producer:	Martin Ransohoff
Cast:	Jack MacGowran (Professor Abronsius), Roman Po-

lanski (Alfred, His Assistant), Alfie Bass (Shagal), Jessie Robins (Rebecca), Sharon Tate (Sarah), Ferdy Mayne (Count Von Krolock), Iain Quarrier (Herbert), Terry Downes (Koukol), Fiona Lewis (Maid), Ronald Lacey (Village Idiot), Sydney Bromley (Sleigh Driver), Andreas Malandrinos, Otto Diamant, Matthew Walters (Woodcutters).

Production: Cadre Films—Filmways, Incorporated

Location scenes filmed in Dolomite Alps, Italy. Released in Great Britain in 1967 as *Dance of the Vampires*; running time of 107 minutes. Producer Martin Ransohoff cut the film for American release from 107 minutes to 98 minutes; also re-dubbed some voices and added animated credit sequence. Polanski disassociates himself from this version.

Distribution: Metro-Goldwyn-Mayer, Incorporated
Running Time: 91 minutes
Released: November 13, 1967
Alternate Titles: *Your Teeth In My Neck, The Vampire Killers, Dance of the Vampires*

15 ROSEMARY'S BABY (1968)

Synopsis

Actor Guy Woodhouse and his wife Rosemary look at an apartment in the Bramford, an elegant old New York City building. Enchanted with what she sees, Rosemary talks Guy into taking the place. Later, however, the Woodhouses are warned against living there by their friend Hutch, who tells them that the building has a bad history involving witchcraft.

Once they have moved in, Rosemary meets a friendly girl called Terry in the laundry room. Terry explains that she lives with the Castevets, an elderly couple who occupy the apartment across the hall from the Woodhouses, and she shows Rosemary a tannis root amulet the Castevets have given her. Subsequently, upon arriving home one evening, Rosemary and Guy notice a crowd around the Bramford and are shocked to discover that Terry has thrown herself out of a window. Following this catastrophe, Minnie Castevet visits Rosemary from time to time and gives her the amulet that Terry wore. Guy, though initially uninterested in the old couple, becomes enthusiastic about them after the Woodhouses go to dinner in the neighboring apartment. Rosemary, however, remains unimpressed. Guy's professional problems unexpectedly come to an end when he is offered a good role previously assigned to an actor who has mysteriously gone blind. Elated by his good fortune, Guy suggests that Rosemary become pregnant, and they plan a special evening together. Rosemary gets groggy from the liquor she has drunk and—she thinks—from eating a chocolate mousse that Minnie Castevet has prepared for them. She falls into a troubled sleep in which she has a vision of being raped by the devil.

Rosemary does become pregnant and, after an initial visit to Dr.

Hill, is cared for by Dr. Sapirstein, an eminent obstetrician recommended by the Castevets. Gradually, she grows more and more suspicious of the people around her, encouraged by Hutch, who believes that Roman Castevet is descended from a well-known Nineteenth Century warlock. However, before Rosemary can meet with Hutch to discuss this sinister possibility, he suddenly dies. Her fears become more intense until, just before the birth of her child, she seeks refuge in the office of Dr. Hill, confiding her suspicions to him. Thinking Rosemary a victim of paranoid delusions, Dr. Hill returns her to Dr. Sapirstein and her husband. But she breaks away from them in the Bramford's elevator and locks herself into her apartment. There she goes into labor and loses consciousness. When the baby is born, she is told that it is dead. Unconvinced, she secretly enters her neighbors' apartment where she finds her child surrounded by a group of Satanists, her husband and the Castevets among them. Explaining to her that the baby is the Devil's son, the Satanists ask Rosemary to be a mother to it. After looking down at the infant in its cradle, she slowly begins to rock it.

Credits and Notes

Producer:	William Castle
Director:	Roman Polanski
Screenplay:	Roman Polanski
Based On Novel By:	Ira Levin
Photography:	William Fraker
Special Effects:	Farciot Edouart
Art Director:	Joel Schiller
Production Designer:	Richard Sylbert
Set Decorator:	Robert Nelson
Music:	Krzysztof Komeda-Trzcinski
Sound:	Harold Lewis, John Wilkinson
Costumes:	Anthea Sylbert
Editors:	Sam O'Steen, Robert Wyman
Assistant Director:	Daniel J. McCauley
Make-Up:	Allan Snyder
Creators of Miss Farrow's Hairstyles:	Sydney Guilaroff, Vidal Sassoon
Hairstylist:	Sherry Wilson
Dialogue Coach:	Howard W. Koch, Jr.
Continuity:	Luanna S. Poole
Production Manager:	William Davidson
Associate Producer:	Dona Holloway
Cast:	Mia Farrow (Rosemary Woodhouse), John Cassavetes (Guy Woodhouse), Ruth Gordon (Minnie Castevet), Sidney Blackmer (Roman Castevet), Maurice Evans (Hutch), Ralph Bellamy (Dr. Sapirstein), Angela Dorian (Terry), Patsy Kelly (Laura-Louise), Elisha Cook (Mr. Nicklas), Emmaline Henry (Elise Dunstan), Marianne Gordon (Joan Jellicoe), Philip Leeds (Dr. Shand), Charles Grodin (Dr. Hill), Hope Sum-

<table>
<tr><td></td><td>mers (Mrs. Gilmore), Wende Wagner (Tiger), Gordon Connell (Guy's Agent), Janet Garland (Nurse), Joan Reilly (Pregnant Woman), Tony Curtis (Voice of Donald Baumgart), William Castle (Man at Telephone Booth), Walter Baldwin, Charlotte Boerner, Sebastian Brook, Ernest Harada, Natalie Masters, Elmer Modlin, Patricia O'Neal, Robert Osterlok, Almira Sessions, Bruno Sidar (Members of the Coven).</td></tr>
</table>

Production:	Paramount/William Castle Enterprises

Exteriors filmed at the Dakota, a well-known New York City apartment building.

Distribution:	Paramount Pictures
Running Time:	137 minutes
Released:	June 12, 1968

Major Awards

David di Donatello Award, Italy, 1968
International Show-A-Rama Award as Director of the Year, 1968
Citation by U. S. Motion Picture Exhibitors' Association as one of Year's Top Ten Filmmakers, 1968

16   MACBETH (1971)

Synopsis

On a deserted beach, three chanting witches bury various objects, including a disembodied hand. On another beach, a battle has ended. Duncan, king of Scotland, passes sentence on the treasonous Thane of Cawdor. Upon hearing of Macbeth's military triumphs, Duncan orders the condemned noble's title bestowed on the victorious warrior. Riding from the scene of the battle, Macbeth and Banquo meet the three witches, who greet Macbeth as Thane of Cawdor and tell him that he will "be king hereafter." They also promise Banquo that he will father kings, though he will not be king himself. Shortly after this encounter, Macbeth is told that he has indeed been named Thane of Cawdor.

At Macbeth's castle, Lady Macbeth reads a letter from her husband that tells of the witches' predictions and their partial fulfillment. She resolves to spur Macbeth on to insure that the rest of the prophecy comes true as well. When Macbeth returns home, the couple prepare for a visit by Duncan, and Lady Macbeth exhorts her husband to use this opportunity to murder the king. After Duncan arrives, Macbeth hesitates, but ultimately stabs the king while he sleeps. Afterwards, however, Macbeth is unnerved by what he has done, and Lady Macbeth is forced to complete their plan by smearing Duncan's sleeping grooms with blood and placing the murder weapons near them. An early morning entourage, led by Macduff, arrives to wake the king. When Duncan is discovered dead, Macbeth kills the grooms, protesting that he has done so out of "fury" at the realization of their guilt. Alarmed by what has happened, Duncan's two sons, Malcolm and Donalbain, flee the country, and Macbeth is crowned king.

While preparations are underway for a banquet hosted by Macbeth at the royal castle, Banquo tells the new king of his intention to ride in the woods with his son Fleance. Jealous of the witches' promise to Banquo and afraid of what he might suspect about Duncan's murder, Macbeth meets with two hired assassins and orders them to slay Banquo and Fleance in the woods. At the scene of the ambush, the assassins are joined by Ross, another Scottish noble, who helps them murder Banquo. However, the three murderers manage to let Fleance escape. Later, at the banquet, Banquo's ghost appears to Macbeth, prompting him to rave insanely at the apparition. Appalled at her husband's behavior, Lady Macbeth tries to calm him, but is eventually forced to ask the guests to depart.

Macbeth returns to the place where he encountered the witches to discover more about his future. He feels he is safe when the witches tell him that he is in no danger "until Birnam wood come to Dunsinane" and that he can never be hurt by any man "of woman born." Back at the castle, Macbeth is greeted by reports about many who are leaving Scotland, including Macduff, who has left his family behind. Outwardly contemptuous of this news, Macbeth nonetheless orders Macduff's family murdered and his castle destroyed, an atrocity engineered by Ross. Lady Macbeth, in the meantime, has begun walking in her sleep, mumbling incoherently about what she and her husband have done.

In England, Malcolm, Macduff and others gather forces to invade their homeland, having been joined by Ross, who has shifted his loyalties. Before the final attack, the armies chop down trees from Birnam wood and use them to conceal their numbers. News of this fulfillment of the witches' prophecy disturbs Macbeth, and he is further upset by news of his wife's suicide. By the time the army enters the castle, all the inhabitants except Macbeth have fled. He, however, fights boldly with Macduff, secure in the witches' pledge of his invulnerability. But Macduff tells the king that he was "from his mother's womb untimely ripped," and soon fatally wounds Macbeth, concluding the battle by beheading him. Ross then places the crown on Malcolm's head. The final scene has Donalbain stopping to talk with the three witches, just as Macbeth had done before him.

Credits and Notes

Producer:	Andrew Braunsberg
Director:	Roman Polanski
Screenplay:	Roman Polanski, Kenneth Tynan
Based on Play By:	William Shakespeare
Photography:	Gil Taylor
Special Effects:	Ted Samuels
Art Director:	Fred Carter
Production Designer:	Wilfrid Shingleton
Set Decorator:	Bryan Graves

Music	Third Ear Band
Sound:	Simon Kaye
Sound Editor:	Jonathan Bates
Sound Re-Recording:	Nolan Roberts
Costumes:	Anthony Mendleson
Choreography:	Sally Gilpin
Editor:	Alastair McIntyre
Assistant Director:	Simon Relph
Second Unit Director:	Hercules Bellville
Fight Director:	William Hobbs
Horse Master:	Jeremy Taylor
Production Adviser:	David W. Orton
Process Consultant:	Richard Vetter
Associate Producer:	Timothy Burrill
Executive Producer:	Hugh M. Hefner
Artistic Advisor:	Kenneth Tynan

Cast: Jon Finch (Macbeth), Francesca Annis (Lady Macbeth), Martin Shaw (Banquo), Nicholas Selby (Duncan), John Stride (Ross), Stephan Chase (Malcolm), Paul Shelley (Donalbain), Terence Bayler (Macduff), Mark Digham (Macduff's Son), Diane Fletcher (Lady Macduff), Andrew Laurence (Lennox), Frank Wylie (Mentieth), Bernard Archard (Angus), Bruce Purchase (Caithness), Keith Chegwin (Fleance), Noel Davis (Seyton), Noelle Rimmington (Young Witch), Maisie MacFarquhar (Blind Witch), Elsie Taylor (First Witch), Vic Abbott (Cawdor), Richard Pearson (Doctor), Michael Balfour (First Murderer), Andrew McCulloch (Second Murderer), Bill Drysdale (King's Groom), Roy Jones (Second King's Groom), Patricia Mason (Gentlewoman), Ian Hogg (First Minor Thane), Geoffrey Reed (Second Minor Thane), Nigel Ashton (Third Minor Thane), Sydney Bromley (Porter), William Hobbs (Young Seyward), Alf Joint (Old Seyward), Howard Lang (First Old Soldier), David Ellison (Second Old Soldier), Terence Mountain (Soldier), Paul Hennen (Boy Apprentice), Beth Owen, Maxine Skelton, Janie Kells, Olga Anthony, Roy Desmond, Pam Foster, John Gordon, Barbara Grimes, Aud Johansen, Dickie Martyn, Christina Paul, Don Vernon, Anna Willoughby (Dancers).

Production: Playboy Productions/ Caliban Films

Exteriors filmed at Bamburgh Castle in Northumberland, Showdonia National Park in Wales, and Lindisfurne Castle on Holy Island. Originally budgeted at $2,400,000; went over budget by $600,000. Original shooting schedule of sixteen weeks; actual schedule of twenty-five weeks.

Distribution:	Columbia Pictures
Running Time:	140 minutes
Released:	December 8, 1971

17 WHAT? [*Che?*] (1973)

Synopsis

Nancy, a naive young American girl hitchhiking in Italy, is beaten and almost raped by a gang of Italian youths one night. She escapes by taking an elevator down to a luxurious villa on the Mediterranean. There she encounters a number of strange characters and records her adventures in a diary she carries with her.

After meeting two servants, an old man and an old woman, the girl spends the night in one of the villa's bedrooms. Upon awakening the next morning, she is dismayed to discover that her T-shirt is missing. Dressed only in her blue jeans, she goes out to the terrace, where she meets Alex, a self-proclaimed pimp. She sits down with him, covering herself by tying a napkin around her neck. Two women, one naked, pass by them without speaking. While drinking coffee, Nancy and Alex talk with two ping-pong players, Tony and Jimmy, who are on the balcony above.

Afterward, back inside the house, the girl finds a pajama top, which she puts on. As she continues to explore the villa and its surroundings, she comes upon Tony and his girlfriend, Lollipop, in a bedroom making love under a rug. Jimmy is on the balcony outside, cooking fish over a barbecue. Soon the aggressive Mosquito appears, wearing Nancy's T-shirt and carrying a harpoon gun, which he calls his "stinger." Later, down at the beach, the girl encounters Pietro, a priest, who suggests that she leave the "decadence and decay" of the villa. Mosquito reappears, first warning her against Alex, then accompanying her to Alex's tower room. There Alex asks Nancy to whip him as he crawls around the floor in a tiger skin. That night, back in her own room again, the girl finds herself displaced by Ruth and Charlie, two American tourists. She goes to sleep on the beach, but awakens to discover her blue jeans missing. She searches for them in Tony and Jimmy's room, then falls asleep in the living room, where she is again disturbed, this time by Giovanni, the manager of the villa, who is looking up her pajama top. She joins him as he plays Mozart on the piano. Returning to Alex's room in the tower, she finds two painters, one of whom inadvertently paints a blue stripe down the back of one of her legs. She then goes to the terrace, where Alex is sitting by the breakfast things. They drink coffee together as on the previous morning. After Alex leaves, Pietro reappears, but is unable to help her when she asks for advice.

At lunch on the terrace, all of the characters are brought together, including Alex's uncle, Joseph Noblart, an art collector and owner of the villa, who is fascinated by Nancy. Alex continues to pursue her as well, and later forces her to play a game with him on the beach in which he, dressed as a policeman, asks her questions and then slaps her brutally when she gives unsatisfactory answers. Back in the house, she is further dismayed to find a group of people reading her diary. After re-enacting her piano playing scene with Giovanni, she is summoned to Noblart's bedroom to indulge the old man's voyeuristic impulses. She inspires such ecstasy in him that he is overcome and dies. Nancy escapes from the room, and her guilty manner causes the others to begin chasing her. With Alex's help, she catches the elevator, after losing her pajama top—her last remaining piece of clothing—to a vicious dog. On the highway, she jumps onto a passing truck full of pigs, waving goodbye to Alex as she rides off into the night.

Credits and Notes

Producer:	Carlo Ponti
Director:	Roman Polanski
Screenplay:	Gerard Brach, Roman Polanski
Photography:	Marcello Gatti, Giuseppe Ruzzolini
Art Director:	Franco Fumagalli
Production Designer:	Aurelio Crugnola
Music (Classics Arranged and Directed):	Claudio Gizzi
Sound:	Piero Fondi
Costumes:	Adriana Berselli
Editor:	Alastair McIntyre
Assistant Director:	Antonio Brandt
Second Unit Director:	Hercules Bellville
Production Manager:	Mara Blasetti
Executive Producer:	Andrew Braunsberg
Cast:	Sydne Rome (Nancy), Marcello Mastroianni (Alex), Hugh Griffith (Joseph Noblart), Romolo Valli (Giovanni), Guido Alberti (Priest), Gianfranco Piacentini (Tony), Roger Middleton (Jimmy), Roman Polanski (Mosquito), Henning Schlueter (Catone), Christine Barry (Dressed Girl), Birgitta Nilsson (Nude Girl), Cicely Brown (Ruth), John Karlsen (Edward), Richard McNamara (Charlie), Elisabeth Witte (Nurse), Dieter Hallervorden (First German), Mogen Von Gadow (Second German), Carlo Delle Piane, Mario Bussolino.
Production:	C. C. Champion (Rome) / Les Films Concordia (Paris) / Dieter Geissler Produktion (Munich)
Distribution:	Avco Embassy Pictures
Running Time:	112 minutes
Released:	October 3, 1973
Alternate Title:	*Diary of Forbidden Dreams*

18 CHINATOWN (1974)

Synopsis

In 1930's Los Angeles, J. J. (Jake) Gittes operates a thriving private detective agency specializing in matrimonial spying. One day, during a city drought, Gittes is called into the office of his employees Walsh and Duffy to confront an unexpectedly important client: Mrs. Hollis Mulwray, the wife of the Los Angeles Water Commissioner. Though Gittes tries to discourage her, Mrs. Mulwray insists that he gather evidence about her husband's infidelity. After following Mulwray for several days, Gittes, Walsh, and Duffy discover that he spends time with a young girl. Gittes takes pictures of the two "lovers" together and gives them to his client. But he discovers shortly afterward that the newspapers have also obtained his information and have created a front page scandal out of it. Immediately after he finds out about this unpleasant publicity, Gittes is confronted in his office by another woman who claims to be the real Mrs. Hollis Mulwray and says that she plans to sue him for libel.

Deeply disturbed by this threat to his professional reputation, Gittes goes to visit Mulwray in his office, but finds him out. He then goes to Mulwray's house, where Evelyn Mulwray greets him cordially and tells him that she no longer wants to prefer charges against him. However, when he continues to insist on seeing her husband, Evelyn suggests that he try looking at the city reservoir. At the reservoir, Gittes meets Lieutenant Lou Escobar, with whom he had past difficulties when both worked on the Los Angeles police force in Chinatown. Escobar is investigating the death of Mulwray, who has drowned in the reservoir. Further examining the situation, Gittes concludes that someone has been tampering with the Los Angeles water supply, thus forcing down the price of farmland so that it can be bought cheaply. The gathering of Gittes's evidence about Mulwray's adultery was part of an attempt to blackmail the Water Commissioner into keeping quiet about the fraud. The detective's suspicions about who was responsible for Mulwray's murder focus on Evelyn when he discovers that she is hiding the girl her husband had been seeing.

Under heavy pressure from Escobar, who suspects that Gittes is shielding Evelyn Mulwray, Gittes forces a showdown with Evelyn, at which point she confesses to him that her husband's "girlfriend" is actually her own daughter, the product of an incestuous affair she had with her father when she was fifteen. Mulwray had been taking care of the girl to keep her away from Evelyn's father, Noah Cross, a very wealthy former business associate of Mulwray. Gittes meets with Cross to accuse him of Mulwray's murder, but Cross brings his hired thugs with him and insists that Gittes take him to his "granddaughter." They find the girl in Chinatown with her mother, ready to leave the city as Escobar, holding Duffy and Walsh in custody, watches. Gittes tries to explain the situation to Escobar, but his accusations against Cross go unheeded; and the police, after ordering Evelyn to stop, shoot and kill her as she drives away with her daughter. As Cross takes charge of the hysterical girl, Escobar tells Gittes to "get out of here," and Walsh tries to console him by saying, "Forget it, Jake; it's Chinatown."

Credits and Notes

Producer:	Robert Evans
Director:	Roman Polanski
Screenplay:	Robert Towne
Photography:	John A. Alonzo
Special Photography:	Logan Frazee
Titles:	Wayne Fitzgerald
Art Director:	W. Stewart Campbell
Production Designer:	Richard Sylbert
Set Designers:	Gabe Resh, Robert Resh
Set Decorator:	Ruby Levitt
Music:	Jerry Goldsmith
Sound Editor:	Robert Cornett
Sound Recording:	Larry Jost
Sound Re-Recording:	Bud Grenzbach
Costumes:	Anthea Sylbert
Editor:	Sam O'Steen
Assistant Directors:	Howard W. Koch, Jr., Michele Ader
Production Manager:	C. O. Erickson
Associate Producer:	C. O. Erickson
Cast:	Jack Nicholson (J. J. Gittes), Faye Dunaway (Evelyn Mulwray), John Huston (Noah Cross), Perry Lopez (Escobar), John Hillerman (Yelburton), Darrell Zwerling (Hollis Mulwray), Diane Ladd (Ida Sessions), Roy Jenson (Mulvihill), Roman Polanski (Man With Knife), Dick Bakalyan (Loach), Joe Mantell (Walsh), Bruce Glover (Duffy), Nandu Hinds (Sophie), James O'Reare (Lawyer), James Hong (Evelyn's Butler), Beulah Quo (Maid), Jerry Fijikawa (Gardener), Belinda Palmer (Katherine), Roy Roberts (Mayor Bagby), Noble Willingham, Elliott Montgomery (Councilmen), Rance Howard (Irate Farmer), George Justin (Barber), Doc Erickson (Customer), Fritzi Burr (Mulwray's Secretary), Charles Knapp (Mortician), Claudio Martinez (Boy on Horseback), Federico Roberto (Cross' Butler), Allan Warnick (Clerk), John Holland, Jesse Vint, Jim Burke, Denny Arnold (Farmers in the Valley), Burt Young (Curly), Elizabeth Harding (Curly's Wife), John Rogers (Mr. Palmer), Cecil Elliott (Emma Dill), Paul Jenkins, Lee DeBroux, Bob Golden (Policemen).
Production:	Long Road Productions; Paramount-Penthouse Presentation

First cameraman Stanley Cortez replaced during filming.

Distribution:	Paramount Pictures
Running Time:	130 minutes
Released:	June 17, 1974

19 THE TENANT [Le Locataire] (1976)

Synopsis

Trelkovsky, a timid Polish filing clerk living in Paris, is having difficulty finding an apartment because of the housing shortage in the city. He hears of a flat that may be available because its former tenant, Simone Choule, has thrown herself out of the living room window and is expected to die. On visiting the building, Trelkovsky decides to take the apartment, although the concierge and the landlord, Monsieur Zy, seem brusque and unfriendly. Before moving in, however, he visits Simone in the hospital. There he meets Stella, a friend of Simone's. Stella becomes so upset by Simone's plight that Trelkovsky offers to take her for a drink to calm her down. After spending some time in a cafe, the two go to the movies, where Stella makes sexual advances to Trelkovsky. He responds tentatively, but they part company upon leaving the theater.

When Simone dies, Trelkovsky moves into his new home. Once there, he discovers that the other tenants in the building are as difficult as the landlord and the concierge. He gives a housewarming party, inviting a rowdy group from his office, and is upbraided by his neighbors for the noise he's caused. Later, upon investigating his new home, Trelkovsky discovers that some of Simone's possessions have been left behind: a dress, nail polish, even a tooth hidden in the wall. Gradually, he comes to believe that the neighbors are engaged in a plot against him; their goal is to turn him into Simone Choule and make him jump out of the window just as she has done. Apprehensively, he observes the other tenants standing motionless by the window of the bathroom across the courtyard, and he expectantly watches as the greenhouse below his apartment, which has been broken by Simone's fall, is repaired. He is further disturbed by the pleas of Mme. Gaderian, another tenant, who wants Trelkovsky to defend her against the persecution of her imperious neighbor, Mme. Dioz. Even the proprietor of the cafe across the street feeds the young filing clerk's growing paranoia by repeatedly confusing his tastes with the tastes of Simone, who had been a regular customer before her death. An unexpected visit from Simone's friend Badar, who has been unaware of her suicide, further disturbs the young Pole's equilibrium.

Trelkovsky's boisterous office companions are unable to lift him out of his black mood, and he becomes increasingly isolated from them. Even a chance meeting with Stella fails to cheer him up for long. Increasingly distraught, he begins to dress up in Simone's clothes, and even pulls out one of his teeth as she had done. During a brief period of relative normalcy, the disoriented clerk seeks refuge at Stella's. She welcomes him, but soon leaves him alone while she goes to work. When an unexpected visitor arrives at her door, Trelkovsky believes that it is Monsieur Zy, and all of his fears are revived. Convinced that Stella, too, is involved in a plot against him, he rampages through her apartment destroying everything he can, and leaves. After wandering the streets awhile, he is struck by a car while fleeing from some imagined tormentors. Only slightly injured, he is taken home by the couple whose car has hit him, his raving condition ascribed to the shock of the accident.

Back at his own lodgings, Trelkovsky's fantasies gain momentum. He dresses up as Simone again and finally jumps from the window as she has done. The shocked neighbors gather around, but Trelkovsky, though gravely wounded, spurns them, for they appear to him as nightmarish monsters. Floundering weakly up the stairs to his apartment, he pushes himself out of the window a second time. We see him next in the hospital, where the earlier scene involving Trelkovsky and Stella at Simone's bedside is repeated. But this time Trelkovsky himself is the bandaged figure in the bed, not Simone, and he gazes in horror at his "other self" standing at the bedside with Stella, finally uttering the same horrifying cry of agony that Simone had given vent to in the earlier scene.

Credits and Notes

Producer:	Andrew Braunsberg
Director:	Roman Polanski
Screenplay:	Gerard Brach, Roman Polanski
Based on the Novel By:	Roland Topor
Photography:	Sven Nykvist, A.S.C.
Camera Operator:	Jean Harnois
Camera Assistants:	Francois Catonne, Bruno DeKeyzer
Optical Effects:	Jean Fouche
Special Photography:	Louma
Art Direction:	Claude Moesching, Albert Rajau
Production Designer:	Pierre Guffroy
Set Decoration:	Eric Simon
Music:	Philippe Sarde
Orchestrations:	Hubert Rostaing, Carlo Savina
Sound Editor:	Michele Boehm
Sound Mixer:	Jean Pierre Ruh
Sound Re-Recording	Jean Neny
Sound Boom Operator:	Louis Gimel
Costumes:	Mimi Gayo
Editor:	Francoise Bonnot
Assistant Editor:	Jacques Audiard
Assistant Director:	Marc Greenbaum
Second Assistant Directors:	Jean Jacques Aublanc, Jean Pierre Poussin
Make-Up:	Didier Labergne
Hairdresser:	Ludovic Paris
Dialogue Director:	Jacques Levy
Continuity:	Sylvette Baudrot

Production Secretary:	Simone Escoffier
Still Photographer:	Bernard Prim
Unit Publicist:	Walter Alford
Props:	Raymond Lemoigne
Casting:	Catherine Vernoux
Production Manager:	Marc Maurette
Unit Managers:	Yves Marin, Juliette Toutain
Associate Producer:	Alain Sarde
Executive Producer:	Hercules Bellville
Recording Studios:	Simo
Cast:	Roman Polanski (Trelkovsky), Isabelle Adjani (Stella), Shelley Winters (The Concierge), Melvyn Douglas (M. Zy), Jo Van Fleet (Mme. Dioz), Bernard Fresson (Scope), Lila Kedrova (Mme. Gaderian), Claude Dauphin (Husband in Car Accident), Claude Pieplu (Apartment Neighbor), Rufus (Badar), Romain Bouteille (Simon), Jacques Monod (Cafe Proprietor), Patrice Alexsandre (Robert), Jean Pierre Bagot (Policeman), Josiane Balasko (Viviane), Michel Blanc (Scope's Neighbor), Florence Blot (Mme. Zy), Louba Chazel (Wife in Car Accident), Jacques Chevalier (Policeman in Car Accident), Jacky Cohen (Friend of Stella), Alain Davis (Doctor in Car Accident).

Credits and Notes: A List

20 *The Bicycle: See* item 1.

21 *A Toothy Smile: See* item 2.

22 *Break Up the Dance: See* item 3.

23 *The Crime: See* item 4.

24 *Two Men and a Wardrobe: See* item 5.

25 *The Lamp: See* item 6.

26 *When Angels Fall: See* item 7.

27 *The Fat and the Lean: See* item 8.

28 *Knife in the Water: See* item 9.

29 *Mammals: See* item 10.

30 *The Beautiful Swindlers: See* item 11.

31 *Repulsion: See* item 12.

32 *Cul-de-Sac: See* item 13.

33 *The Fearless Vampire Killers . . . : See* item 14.

34 *Rosemary's Baby: See* item 15.

35 *Macbeth: See* item 16.

36 *What?: See* item 17.

37 *Chinatown: See* item 18.

38 *The Tenant: See* item 19.

Major Awards: A List

39 *Two Men and a Wardrobe*: *See* item 5.

40 *Knife in the Water*: *See* item 9.

41 *Mammals*: *See* item 10.

42 *Repulsion*: *See* item 12.

43 *Cul-de-Sac*: *See* item 13.

44 *Rosemary's Baby*: *See* item 15.

Annotated Guide to
Writings About the Director

1958

45   Butcher, Mary Vonne. "Films and Freedom: Creativity Despite Repression." *Commonweal*, 69, no. 3 (17 October), 65–66.
Very brief review of *Two Men and a Wardrobe*.

*46   Queval, Jean. "*Deux Hommes et Une Armoire*." *Téléciné*, nos. 75/76.
Cited in Belmans. *See* No. 346.

47   Reisz, Karel. "The Festivals Experiment at Brussels." *Sight and Sound*, 27, no. 5 (Summer), 231–34.
Very brief review of *Two Men and a Wardrobe* as the "revelation of the Festival." Illustrated.

48   Thirifays, André. "*Deux Hommes et Une Armoire*." *Le Soir*, no. 121 (2 May), p. 20.
Reviewer praises this small "admirable" black comedy which "evokes too well the sad witness of our world: Kafka."

1959

49   Harker, Jonathan. "*Two Men and a Wardrobe*." *Film Quarterly*, 12, no. 3 (Spring), 53–55.
Review calls film "best thing of its kind in thirty years" because of the way it "juggles symbol and reality." After initially establishing its "preposterous premise," it presents what follows in a "detached, logical fashion." A wide angle shot when Polanski himself advances, his fists in front of him, is the film's "single visual error."

1960

50   Costes, Claude. "Entretien avec Raymond Polanski." *Positif*, no. 33, pp. 12–15.
Polanski's first interview in a French magazine centers on his initial work in films as an actor in Poland and his studies at the École Supérieure de Cinéma in Lodz.

1961

*51 Oleksiewicz, Maria. "Troje Ludzi Na Jachcie. Reportaz z Realizacji Filmu *Nóż W Wodzie." Film*, no. 36, pp. 10–11.
Cited by Filmoteka Polska; *See* No. 681.

1962

52 Anon. *Contemporary Polish Cinematography, A Collective Work.* Warsaw: Polonia Publishing House, pp. 54, 73.
Brief mention of *Two Men and a Wardrobe* praising "its poetic atmosphere, the pinch of honey and a logical and simple narrative." Illustrated.

53 Baby, Yvonne. "Au Festival du court métrage de Tours la Pologne . . ." *Le Monde* (12 December), p. 16.
Very brief review of *Mammals*, "one of the privileged moments of the Festival."

54 Beylin, Stefania. *"Nóż W Wodzie." Glos Nauczycielski*, no. 13, p. 6.
In *Knife in the Water*, Polanski creates the necessary atmosphere and holds attention, but the film is unsuitable for young people in its pessimism.

*55 Braun, Andrzej. *"Nóż W Wodzie." Film*, no. 12, pp. 4–5.
Cited by Filmoteka Polska; *See* No. 681.

56 Bryll, Ernest. *"Nóż W Wodzie." Wspólczesność*, no. 7, p. 5.
Polanski accurately portrays the rituals of the "now" age in the well-made *Knife in the Water*.

*57 Chevalier, J. *"Le Gros et le Maigre." Image et Son*, no. 147.
Cited in Belmans. *See* No. 346.

58 Collective Work. *La Cinématographie Polonaise.* Warsaw: Polonia Publishing House.
Translated in No. 52.

59 Douchet, Jean. "Venise 1962." *Cahiers du Cinéma*, no. 136 (October), p. 43.
Very brief mention of the "very interesting" *Knife in the Water*, "a satire without pity."

*60 Davay, Paul. *"Le Gros et le Maigre." Programme de l'Ecran du Séminaire des Arts* (11 December).
Cited in Belmans. *See* No. 346.

61 Gilliatt, Penelope. *"Knife in the Water." London Observer* (14 October), p. 29.
Very brief review of film as "a scalding piece of original film-making."

62 Grzelecki, Stanislaw. *"Nóż W Wodzie." Życie Warszawy*, no. 60, 8.
Reviewer finds *Knife in the Water* boring and unoriginal, worthy of comment only because of Polanski's organization and the fact that it's Polish.

63   J. J. S. "*Nóż W Wodzie.*" *Tygodnik Powszechny,* no. 14, p. 8.
      Knife in the Water is an "ambitious" film revealing intuition and imagina-
      tion, but lacking continuity of motivation.

*64   Kalużyński, Zygmunt. "*Nóż W Wodzie.*" *Polityka,* no. 11, p. 8.
      Cited by Filmoteka Polska; *See* No. 681.

65   Klaczyński, Zbigniew. "*Nóż W Wodzie.*" *Trybuna Ludu,* no. 69, p. 8.
      Polanski's *Knife in the Water* exposes the moral poverty of its characters;
      exploring not "who" but "how" they are, in "the best Polish film of the
      French New Wave."

66   Kochański, Kazimierz. "*Nóż W Wodzie.*" *Tygodnik Kulturalny,* no.
      12, p. 8.
      Review finds *Knife in the Water* uninteresting emptiness which is not
      redeemed by Polanski's technical abilities.

67   Kydryński, Juliusz. "*Nóż W Wodzie.*" *Zycie Literackie,* no. 13, p. 9.
      Kydryński concludes that *Knife in the Water* shows talent although the
      dialogue is "narrow" and the characters unsympathetic.

*68   Manturzewski, Stanislaw. "Bo Ja Wiem . . .? Próba Paszkwilu Na
      '*Nóż W Wodzie.*' " *Film,* no. 14, p. 7.
      Cited by Filmoteka Polska; *See* No. 681.

69   Marroncle, Jeanine. "Venise." *Téléciné,* no. 107 (October-November).
      Brief review of *Knife in the Water* calls it a "small masterpiece."

70   Michalek, Boleslaw. "*Nóż W Wodzie.*" *Nowa Kultura,* no. 12, p. 8.
      Michalek feels that, although not overly moralistic, *Knife in the Water*
      fails to show life with all its surprises and unequal but free movement.

71   Michalski, Czeslaw. "*Nóż W Wodzie.*" *Walka Mlodyck,* no. 11, p. 15.
      In *Knife in the Water,* Polanski reveals his masterful direction in his
      original and interesting handling of a restricted narrative situation.

72   Oleksiewicz, Maria. "O Polskim '*Nożu W Wodzie*' Na Tle Francuskiej
      'Nowej Fali,'" *Film,* no. 12, pp. 10–11.
      Polanski discusses *Knife in the Water,* its characters and psychological
      conflict, in relation to the French New Wave.

73   Plażewski, Jerzy. "*Nóż W Wodzie.*" *Przeglad Kulturalny,* no. 12, p. 8.
      Although *Knife in the Water* reflects excellent continuity of style, dialogue,
      and organization, Plażewski criticizes Polanski's use of amateurs.

*74   Raczkowski, Jerzy. "*Nóż W Wodzie,*" *Wież,* no. 5, pp. 176–79.
      Cited by Filmoteka Polska; *See* No. 681.

*75   Redycki, Edmund. "*Nóż W Wodzie.*" *Kierunki,* no. 11, p. 10.
      Cited by Filmoteka Polska; *See* No. 681.

76   Salachas, Gilbert. "Tours 1961." *Téléciné,* no. 101 (January).
      Brief review of *The Fat and the Lean* calls it "perplexing but moving."

***77**   Sawicki, Andrzej. *"Nóż W Wodzie." Jazz*, no. 5, p. 15.
Cited by Filmoteka Polska; *See* No. 681.

78   Toeplitz, K. T. *"Nóż W Wodzie." Świat*, no. 12, p. 19.
Review of *Knife in the Water* praises portrayal of generational conflict, but finds presentation of exotic situation unconvincing and "cold."

79   Torok, Jean-Paul. "Tours 61." *Positif*, no. 44, p. 58.
Very brief mention of *The Fat and the Lean*, "disappointing in its ambiguity."

80   Tylczyński, Andrzej. *"Nóż W Wodzie." Tygodnik Demokratyczny*, no. 12, p. 8.
In spite of the performance of Leon Niemczyk (husband), *Knife in the Water* is an unconvincing portrayal of society as "owner-fools" and youths aspiring to that role.

81   Walasek, Mieczyslaw. "Apokalipsa We Troje." *Ekran*, no. 11, p. 7.
Although *Knife in the Water* is "spellbinding" and attempts to counter negative tendencies of cowardice, immorality, and egoism in Poland, Walasek finds the film "shocking" in its nihilistic world view.

1962–1963

82   Dyer, Peter John. "Life's a Pain Anyway." *Sight and Sound*, 32 (Winter), 23.
Review of *Knife in the Water* with its theme of "sterility that hides behind meaningless bourgeois poses," praises Polanski as a "holy terror of intelligent restraint" but ultimately faults the film as lacking humanity. Illustrated.

1963

83   Alpert, Hollis. "From the School at Lodz." *Saturday Review*, 46 (26 October), 51.
Review includes background on film production unit for *Knife in the Water* at the Polish National Film Academy which allowed Polanski great freedom in producing a technically skilled and accomplished film, marred only by its almost "too fashionable" surface.

84   Anon. "A Fork In The Road." *Newsweek*, 62 (4 November), 102.
Although the surface of *Knife in the Water* appears taut and "flawless," Polanski's avoidance of a final choice at the end between "social reality" or "domestic reality" finally diminishes his characters' relevance. Illustrated.

85   Anon. *"Knife in the Water." Filmfacts*, 6, no. 44 (5 December), 269–71.
Brief plot synopsis and excerpts from reviews in *The New York Herald Tribune, Time, New York Times, Saturday Review, Variety*, and *The New Republic*. Illustrated.

86   Anon. *"Knife in the Water." Films and Filming*, 9, no. 5 (February), 52.
Photo-essay.

87 Ayfre, Amédée. "Tours 1962." *Téléciné,* no. 109 (February-March).
Brief review of *Mammals* praises its blend of realism and abstraction, its
humor, its plasticity, and its sense of movement.

88 Baker, Peter. "*Nóż W Wodzie.*" *Film and Filming,* 9, no. 5 (February), 52.
Photo essay of stills from *Knife in the Water.*

89 Baroncelli, Jean. "*Le Couteau Dans L'Eau.*" *Le Monde* (26 April),
p. 16.
"Badly titled, but an extremely engaging film," *Knife in the Water* contains an "acuteness of style, a subtlety, a suppleness in the guidance of
the narration" which places Polanski among the most brilliant representatives of the Polish "new wave."

*90 Belmans, Jacques. "Jeune École Polonaise: Roman Polanski." *Rencontre,* no. 3/4.
Cited in Belmans. *See* No. 346.

91 Crowther, Bosley. "Exposing the Obscure." *New York Times* (10
November), II, p. 1.
Comments on letter from reader about sexual symbolism in *Knife in the
Water* objects that movie is "scant."

92 Crowther, Bosley. "Festival Films." *New York Times* (3 November), II, p. 1.
Brief appraisal of films screened at New York festival calls *Knife in the
Water* a "compact, precocious exercise."

93 Crowther, Bosley. "*Knife in the Water.*" *New York Times* (29 October), p. 31.
Review objects to film's "purposeful monotony," but praises "engaging"
performances and theme of "men asserting their egos" in modern world.
Illustrated. Reprinted in No. 334.

*94 Dardenne, J. C. "*Le Couteau Dans L'Eau.*" *Le Peuple* (31 May).
Cited in Belmans. *See* No. 346.

*95 Davay, Paul. "*Le Couteau Dans L'Eau.*" *Les Beaux-Arts* (7 June).
Cited in Belmans. *See* No. 346.

*96 Davay, Paul. "*Deux Hommes et Une Armoire.*" *Programme de
l'Ecran du Séminaire des Arts* (2 April).
Cited in Belmans. *See* No. 346.

97 Ford, Renée. "Interpretation." *New York Times* (17 November),
II, p. 9.
Letter about *Knife in the Water* by Polanski's interpreter at the New York
Film Festival quotes him as denying the sexual symbolism in the film and
emphasizing the different "economic positions" of the two men.

98 Gill, Brendan. "Fun Afloat." *New Yorker,* 39 (2 November), 195.
Very brief review of *Knife in the Water* as an anecdote surprising in its
"brisk, fresh, harsh playfulness."

99 Gilson, René. *"Le Couteau Dans L'Eau." Cinéma 63* [Paris], no. 77 (June), pp. 126–27.

Review praises Polanski's "Bergmanian" unveiling of his characters' inner lives and his expert filming, which never calls attention to itself.

100 Greeley, Bill. "A Pole Looks at Capitalistic TV." *Variety* (2 October), pp. 32, 52.

Brief interview in which Polanski complains that American TV is too "theatrical" and compares it to TV in Poland.

101 Hartung, Philip. "Scalene." *Commonweal*, 79 (8 November), 195.

Brief review of *Knife in the Water* finds it "fascinates even while it repels" with its dim view of humanity.

102 Hatch, Robert. "Films." *Nation*, 197 (30 November), 373.

Very brief review of *Knife in the Water* as "a moral tale with tongue in cheek" which "fully exploits the compelling sensuosity of the screen."

103 Haudiquet, Philippe. "Nouveaux Cinéastes Polonais: Roman Polanski." *Premier Plan*, no. 27, pp. 123–31.

Special edition contains background on Polish cinema and brief biographical notes, filmographies, and notes on films (often drawn from other reviews) of eight Polish filmmakers, including the "young turbulent genius" of Roman Polanski whose "talent, sensitivity and profound originality" are evident through his early works.

104 Kauffmann, Stanley. "Discovery of the Pole." *The New Republic*, 149 (2 November), 30.

Review characterizes *Knife in the Water* as "a small Sartrean system of tensions and countertensions rooted in character" and praises it as "visually rich," though occasionally in need of tighter editing. Reprinted in No. 212.

*105 Lefebur, Pierre. *La Cité* (24 April, 31 May).
Cited in Belmans. *See* No. 346.

*106 Lobet, Marcel. *"Mammifères." Le Soir* (1 June).
Cited in Belmans. *See* No. 346.

*107 Louis, Théodore. *"Le Couteau Dans L'Eau." La Libre Belgique* (31 May).
Cited in Belmans. *See* No. 346.

108 McVay, Douglas. *"Knife in the Water." Film* [England], no. 35 (Spring), p. 26.

Brief review calls film "an exciting advance" over Polanski's previous work in its more realistic portrayal of psychology, conveying the point that "all men are basically aggressors and destroyers."

109 March, Sibyl. *"Knife in the Water." The Seventh Art*, 2, no. 1 (Winter), 6–8, 29.

All Polanski's films are sado-masochistic, and the conflict in *Knife in the Water* "is one of masculinity," with Christine as "the prize." The movie "hints that Andrzej may be impotent," and the outcome proves that youth "must inevitably triumph." Polanski "has made an absorbing but totally detached film about people he dislikes," one which "condemns the tendencies of the society which shaped them." Following the article is a brief question-and-answer article with the director focusing on the filmmaking scene in Poland. Illustrated.

110 Marcuse, Dr. Donald J. "Mailed Opinions." *New York Times* (17 November), II, p. 9.
Psychiatrist analyzes *Knife in the Water* as a study of "Oedipal . . . rivalry."

111 Martin, Marcel. "Le Rimbaud du Court Métrage." *Cinéma 63* [Paris], no. 73, p. 60.
Brief review of *Mammals* compares Polanski to Chaplin and Brecht and praises him as a master of the short film. Illustrated.

°112 Michaux, Willy. "*Mammifères.*" *Drapeau Rouge Magazine* (1 June).
Cited in Belmans. *See* No. 346.

113 Quigley, Isabel. "One of Three." *The Spectator*, 210 (25 January), 99.
Brief review praises "tight, cold, vivid, functional style" of the "brilliantly successful" *Knife in the Water* which investigates psychological truths "through visual intensity."

114 Sarris, Andrew. "Films." *The Village Voice*, 9, no. 2 (31 October), 13.
Brief review of *Knife in the Water* calls it "an aquatic parody of the Hemingway safari and moment-of-truth genre," but objects to its "sour Americanoid jazz score."

°115 Seidl, Peter. "Fiche D'Analyse avec Découpage Plan par Plan." *Étude*, no. 17.
Cited in Belmans. *See* No. 346.

°116 Skwara, Janusz. "Polanski." *Film*, no. 11, pp. 10–11.
Cited by Filmoteka Polska; *See* No. 681.

°117 Thonon, Pierre and Maggy. "*Le Couteau Dans L'Eau.*" *L'Echo de la Bourse* (30 May).
Cited in Belmans. *See* No. 346.

118 Torok, Jean-Paul. "Prélude à Polanski." *Positif*, nos. 50/51/52 (March), pp. 38–40.
Discussion of Polanski, "the author of many cinematographic fables of disconcerting composition and enigmatic morality," and his work, focuses on his first full-length feature, *Knife in the Water*, in which "the formalism of the 'mise en scène' reflects a moral attitude," a pessimistic world view which presents the true nature of his protagonists as transformed by the intrigue of human relations into "puppets without souls."

119 Torok, Jean-Paul. "Tours." *Positif*, no. 53 (June), p. 49.
Very brief review of *Mammals*.

120 Weiler, A. H. "View From a Local Vantage Point." *New York Times* (27 October), II, p. 9.

Brief interview with Polanski about his plans to film Beckett's *Waiting for Godot, Cherchez La Femme* and *If Katelbach Arrives (Cul-De-Sac).*

121 Weyergans, François. "Les certitudes sensibles." *Cahiers du Cinéma,* no. 144 (June), pp. 42–44.

Article discusses *Knife in the Water* in Kantian terms concerning the filming of fragments of daily existence, a "little idiotic and insignificant" which in brief moments remind us of destiny and fortune, and which the author praises as a cinema which "comes to terms with sensible certainties."

1963–1964

122 Gaussen, Fréderic. "*Le Couteau Dans L'Eau.*" *Téléciné,* nos. 113/114 (December-January), pp. 1–8.

Article includes brief Polanski biography and filmography, and synopsis, analysis of mis en scène, music, characters, and themes of *Knife in the Water,* which has the style "of a fable (an apparent jest, with tragic undertones) . . . a specialty of Polanski." Illustrated.

123 Weinberg, Gretchen. "Interview with Roman Polanski." *Sight and Sound,* 33, no. 1 (Winter), 32–33.

Polanski discusses his background, filmmaking in Poland, his development of films out of a "mood," and the importance of visuals, in particular in relationship to *Knife in the Water.* Illustrated.

1964

124 Anon. "*Knife in the Water (Nóż W Wodzie).*" *International Film Guide,* edited by Peter Cowie, vol. 1. London: Tantivy and New York: A. S. Barnes, pp. 92–93.

Brief review praises film's "lonely setting," "superb acting," and "brilliant script, full of intellectual sparring between the two men." Illustrated.

125 Anon. "Polish film director on the way up." *The Times* [London] (8 April), p. 10.

Brief profile with quotes from Polanski, who was on his way to Hollywood for the Academy Awards Ceremony.

126 Anon. "Wstret! Polańskiego." *Film* [Warsaw], no. 46 (15 November).

Repulsion represents a clinically correct portrayal of the psychological disintegration of the central character according to a famous psychiatrist.

127 Billard, Pierre. "*Les Plus Belles Escroqueries Du Monde.*" *Cinéma 64* [Paris], no. 89 (September-October), p. 116.

Brief review praises Polanski's skill in making short films.

128 Bontemps, J[acques]. "*Les Plus Belles Escroqueries du Monde.*" *Cahiers du Cinéma,* no. 159 (October), pp. 70-71.

Brief review of "River of Diamonds" segment, directed with a "surety of craft." Illustrated.

129 Cohn, Bernard. "Oberhausen 64." *Positif*, no. 60 (April-May), p. 63.
Very brief review of *When Angels Fall*.

130 Grenier, Cynthia. "Parisian Panorama." *New York Times* (22 March),
II, p. 11.
A brief news account of the production of *Aimez-Vous Les Femmes?*,
scenario by Polanski.

131 Haudiquet, Philippe. *"Quand Les Anges Tombent." Image et Son*,
nos. 170/171 (February-March), pp. 168–71.
See No. 132.

132 Haudiquet, Philippe. "Roman Polanski." *Image et Son*, nos. 170/171
(February-March), pp. 168–71.
Background material on the films made at Lodz preface discussion of
The Fat and the Lean, Knife in the Water and *Mammals*, three films which
show the "blossoming" of the full talent of the director. Illustrated.

133 Miller, Jonathan. "3½." *New York Review of Books*, 11, no. 1 (20
February), 11–12.
Brief review considers *Knife in the Water* not only as a "stylish three-
finger exercise on the theme of pride" in its eternal sexual triangle, but also
as an examination of the political questions about the right to property.

134 Polanski, Roman. "Roman Polanski." *Cinéma 64* [Paris] *Spécial:
Dix Ans de Cinéma Français*, p. 81.
Brief statement by the director on the absolute necessity for mastery of
film technique among New Wave directors.

135 Silke, James. *"Knife in the Water." Cinema* [Los Angeles], 2, no. 1
(February), 47.
Brief review praises film's "sensuous" quality and its "natural, poetic
camerawork." Illustrated.

136 Wachowicz, Barbara. "O Nowym Filmie Romana Polanskiego."
Przekroj, no. 1024, p. 14.
Polanski discusses *Repulsion* and his "obsession" for filming women with
obsessions.

137 Watts, Stephen. "Britain's Screen Scene." *New York Times* (15
November), II, p. 13.
A brief account of production details on background and filming of
Repulsion.

1965

138 Alpert, H[ollis]. "The Headstrong Directors." *Saturday Review*, 48
(16 October), 63.
Reviewer praises Polanski's direction of *Repulsion* as "brilliantly executed,
stark and absorbing," but feels that he overreached himself in the use of
some effects to produce a shocker to "out-Hitchcock Hitchcock."

139 Anon. "A Maiden Berserk." *Time*, 86 (8 October), 115.
Review praises *Repulsion* as a "nightmare mosaic" created by "an imaginative and perverse master of the dark art of menaces" but wonders if it "serves any purpose other than to scare people silly." Illustrated.

140 Anon. "Ambitious film that misses its mark." *The Times* [London] (10 June), p. 7.
Brief review of *Repulsion* objects to its "pretensions."

141 Anon. "*Repulsion*." *Movie*, no. 13 (Summer), p. 44.
Very brief review of *Repulsion*, as the "sexual hallucinations of a young girl."

142 Anon. "*Repulsion*." *Vogue*, 146 (December), 147.
Repulsion "ingeniously put together," but ultimately empty technique.

143 Anon. "*Ssaki (Mammals)*." *Monthly Film Bulletin*, 32, no. 378 (July), 115.
Brief review sees film as "less masochistic" than *Le Gros et le Maigre*, but "thinner" in substance.

144 Barr, Charles. "*Repulsion*." *Movie*, no. 14 (Fall), pp. 26–27.
Comparison of relations between *Psycho* and *Repulsion* in use of the attraction-repulsion concept in an "oppressive and disturbing film."

145 Bagh, Peter von. "*Repulsion*." *Movie*, no. 14 (Fall), pp. 27–28.
Repulsion discussed as a film of social criticism: "exceptionally interesting, penetrating and also funny, because of certain sexual aberrations, the roots of which lie deep in everyday life." Illustrated.

*146 Botermans, Jan. "*Répulsion*." *Week-End* (20, 25 November).
Cited in Belmans. *See* No. 346.

147 Crowther, Bosley. "Movie On Insanity By Pole Opens At N. Y. Theatre." *New York Times* (4 October), p. 7.
Review calls *Repulsion* one of the best films of the year, praising its "haunting concept of the pain and pathos of the mentally deranged." Reprinted in No. 335.

*148 Davay, Paul. "*Répulsion*." *Les Beaux-Arts* (4 November).
Cited in Belmans. *See* No. 346.

*149 Debongnie, Jean. "Cinéaste à Suivre: Roman Polanski." *La Metropole* (22 October).
Cited in Belmans. *See* No. 346.

*150 Debongnie, Jean. "*Répulsion*." *Amis du Film et de la T.V.*, no. 114 (November).
Cited in Belmans. *See* No. 346.

151 Delahaye, Michel. "Petit Journal du Cinema: *Répulsion*." *Cahiers du Cinéma*, no. 171 (October), pp. 12–13.
Brief review calls film the first cinematic treatment of age-old human sexual obsessions and fears. Illustrated.

152 Durgnat, Raymond. *"Repulsion." Films and Filming*, 11, no. 11 (August), 28–29.

"An admirable compromise between a conventional and a 'stream of consciousness' film," *Repulsion* gives a "vivid picture of being mad" more effectively than any movie made on the subject because it focuses on "all the little failures of contact." It fails only in that "Polanski's detachment tends to underplay the pain and struggle of the sane part of the girl's mind." Illustrated.

*153 Dutrieux, G. *"Répulsion." Le Peuple* (28 October).

Cited in Belmans. *See* No. 346.

154 Dyer, Peter J[ohn]. *"Répulsion." Sight and Sound*, 34, no. 3 (Summer), 146.

Review praises film's "visual elegance" and calls it "clinically persuasive," but finds it ultimately "an irresponsible fiction, compounded of chic reticence, sundry melodramatics . . . and an overall rhythm that is intolerably lethargic and pretentious." Illustrated.

155 Fieschi, Jean-André. *"Répulsion." Cahiers du Cinéma*, no. 168 (July), p. 69.

Brief review considers film as a study in the "poetic" presentation of "wild emotions." Illustrated.

156 Gill, Brendan. "Many Sufferers." *The New Yorker*, 41 (9 October), 190.

Very brief review of the "morbid thriller" *Repulsion* calls it an homage to Hitchcock without his tongue-in-cheek manner to alleviate the boredom.

157 Gregor, Ulrich. *"Répulsion." Cinéma 65* [Paris], no. 99 (September-October), pp. 131–32.

Brief review praises Polanski's depiction of psychology and sees Carol's breakdown as the result of "living in a universe dominated by men." The theme of repulsion is seen as important in all of Polanski's films.

158 Hartung, Philip. "Pathological Path." *Commonweal*, 83 (29 October), 124–25.

Although the reviewer finds the violence and disorder trend in films "alienating," he considers *Repulsion* a skillfully made, believable exercise in Grand Guignol, "shocking and hard to take, but as cinema it is outstanding."

159 Hull, David S. *"Knife in the Water." Film Society Review*, 2 (January), 14.

Brief review praises "variety of meaning" in film and comments on its lack of "propaganda content." Illustrated.

160 Kauffmann, Stanley. "End of an Epoch?" *New Republic*, 153 (16 October), 31–32.

Polanski's film *Knife in the Water* is an example of P. A. Sorokin's claim that modern art is "sensate" and therefore "decadent." Though its Freudianism is clichéd, it is well made. But it may represent, for the director, "a first step down a path of essentially sterile, superb professionalism."

161 Kelly, John. *"Répulsion." Revue Internationale du Cinéma,* no. 94 September), p. 2.
"Roman Polanski is capable of making a truly very important film, but it is not *Repulsion,"* as it finally remains a psychological case study.

162 Kiener, François. "Pour Polanski." *Cinéma 65* [Paris], no. 101, pp. 119–21.
Short article discusses the "different," but "significant" work of the short film, including *When Angels Fall* and *Two Men and a Wardrobe.*

*163 Lefebur, Pierre. *"Répulsion." La Cité* (21 October).
Cited in Belmans. *See* No. 346.

164 Lefèvre, Raymond. *"Les Plus Belles Escroqueries du Monde." Image et Son,* nos. 180/181 (January-February), p. 214.
Brief appraisal singles out Polanski's "River of Diamonds" episode as the only one of interest.

165 Lobet, Marcel. *"Répulsion." Le Soir* (29 October).
According to this brief review the spectator of *Repulsion* "oscillates between nightmare and reality, but also between admiration and repulsion. . . ." Illustrated.

*166 Louis, Théodore. *"Les Plus Belles Escroqueries du Monde." La Libre Belgique* (16 July).
Cited in Belmans. *See* No. 346.

*167 Louis, Théodore. *"Répulsion." La Libre Belgique* (21 October).
Cited in Belmans. *See* No. 346.

*168 Paris, André. *"Les Plus Belles Escroqueries du Monde." Le Soir* (16 July).
Cited in Belmans. *See* No. 346.

169 Plażewski, Jerzy. "Odraza." *Film,* no. 27, p. 3.
Repulsion skillfully analyzes and presents a descent into paranoia. However, the film presents scenes of the macabre even Luis Bunuel "could hardly take."

170 Sarris, Andrew. *"Repulsion; The Ipcress File; The Hours of Love." The Village Voice* (7 October), p. 27.
Review objects to "subjective surrealism" of film's fantasy sequences, but claims that its "triumphs of suspense" make up for it. Reprinted in No. 340.

*171 Tatarkiewicz, Anna. "I Co Dalej?" *Ekran,* no. 27, p. 7.
Cited by Filmoteka Polska; *See* No. 681.

172 Thompson, Howard. "The Road to *Repulsion." New York Times* (14 November), II, p. 9.
Interview with Polanski on the background and the making of *Repulsion.* Illustrated.

*173 Thonon, Pierre and Maggy. *"Répulsion." L'Echo de la Bourse* (1 October).
Cited in Belmans. *See* No. 346.

174 Tynan, Kenneth. "A Grisly Tour de Force of Sex and Suspense." *Life*, 59 (8 October), 23.
Repulsion "establishes Polanski as a master of the casual macabre." Though it suffers from a weak script, it shows the director's "cinematic flair and image-juggling virtuosity." It is *"Psycho* turned inside out."

*175 Van Kerkhoven, Jan. *"Les Plus Belles Escroqueries du Monde." Film* [Belgium], no. 51 (January).
Cited in Belmans. *See* No. 346.

1966

176 Alpert, Hollis. "Know The Enemy." *Saturday Review*, 49 (10 December), 65.
Reviewer supports awarding of Golden Bear at Berlin to *Cul-De-Sac* for Polanski's skill at cinematic storytelling in presenting his "comical and at times nightmarish vision."

177 Anon. "Nearly a thriller in the grand manner." *The Times* [London] (2 June), p. 19.
Brief review of *Cul-De-Sac* sees Polanski's direction as "full of empty gestures."

178 Anon. News Announcement. *The Times* [London] (8 July), p. 18.
Tells of Golden Bear Award to *Cul-De-Sac* at the Berlin Film Festival.

179 Anon. "On the Scene." *Playboy*, 13, no. 10 (October), 162.
Brief biography. Illustrated.

180 Anon. "Razor-Edged Slapstick." *Time*, 88 (18 November), 122–24.
Review of *Cul-De-Sac* praises "tension" between performers and Polanski's "razor-edge" slapstick. Illustrated.

181 Anon. *"Repulsion." International Film Guide*, edited by Peter Cowie. Vol. 3. London: Tantivy and New York: A. S. Barnes, p. 84.
Brief review praises Polanski's talent for "defining the sinister elements of physical objects" but finds many scenes "gratuitous, old-fashioned and derivative."

*182 Aubriant, Michel. *"Cul-De-Sac." Le Nouveau Candide* (12 September).
Cited in Belmans. *See* No. 346.

*183 Baroncelli, Jean. *"Répulsion." Le Monde* (9 October).
Cited in Belmans. *See* No. 346.

184 Benayoun, Robert. "Cannes Vingt: Olé!" *Positif*, no. 79 (October), pp. 82–84.

Reviewer praises *Cul-De-Sac* as "simply his best film, which unites the humor and the sense of the grotesque of his best short films with the implacable skill of *Repulsion*." Illustrated.

185　Bontemps, Jacques. "Du Paradoxe au Lieu Commun." *Cahiers du Cinéma*, no. 176 (March), pp. 77–78.
Brief review of Polanski's short, *When Angels Fall*. Reprinted in No. 186.

186　Bontemps, Jacques. "From the Paradox to the Commonplace." *Cahiers du Cinéma in English*, no. 4, pp. 59-60.
Reprint of No. 185.

*187　Bory, Jean-Louis. "*Cul-De-Sac*." *Le Nouvel Observateur* (30 November-6 December).
Cited in Belmans. See No. 346.

188　Brach, Gérard. "Polanski Via Brach." *Cinéma 65* [Paris], no. 93, pp. 27, 29.
Polanski's co-scenarist discusses his methods of working with the director, focusing on the screenplays of *Repulsion* and *Cul-De-Sac*. Polanski's Slavonic temperament drew him to the subject matter of *Repulsion* in which the girl's motivations are "always sexual." Polanski likes to "improvise during shooting." *Cul-De-Sac* was the screenplay that "satisfied us most," because it "opposed the characters to the environment" most effectively. Illustrated.

189　Caen, Michel. "Victim and Executioner." *Cahiers du Cinéma in English*, no. 4, pp. 56–57.
Reprint of No. 190.

190　Caen, Michel. "Victime et Bourreau." *Cahiers du Cinéma*, no. 176 (March), 72.
Review of *Repulsion*, "a work of pure terror," with reference to the legacy of Hitchcock in the "noble" work of creating fear. Illustrated. Reprinted in No. 189.

*191　Cervoni, Albert. *Dictionnaire du Cinema*. Paris: Universitaires Edition.
Cited in Belmans. See No. 346.

192　Ciment, Michel. "Venise 66." *Image et Son*, no. 199 (November), p. 81.
Brief review of *Cul-De-Sac* calls film a "total success" by a director who has remained true to his obsessions.

193　Clouzot, Claire. "*Répulsion*." *Cinéma 66* [Paris], no. 103, pp. 109–10.
In spite of his borrowings from past horror films, Polanski has managed to combine in *Repulsion* "a refined taste" with "gross, nightmarish" material. Initially, he focuses on a bland setting and the "inexpressive" face of Catherine Deneuve. But the film goes on to explore "Carol's ethic" which postulates that "everything that emanates from women is healthy, and everything masculine is disgusting." The details used to express Carol's madness, however, are clichéd.

194 Cohn, Bernard. *"Répulsion."* *Positif*, no. 75 (May), pp. 133–36.
Although certain parts of the film may shock, the author feels that understanding comes from attention to structure and the smallest detail, for every element of *Repulsion* is essential to the "grand precision" of the total film; directed with an "astonishing surety of technique in the murder scenes . . . unusual in a young director." Illustrated.

195 Crist, Judith. "Idle Dreams About Idols." *World Journal Tribune* (20 November).
Polanski's great talent, "the pure cinematic eye" exhibited in *Knife in the Water* and *Repulsion* is wasted on the pointless, grotesque material of *Cul-De-Sac*. Reprinted in No. 274.

196 Crowther, Bosley. *"Cul-De-Sac."* *New York Times* (8 November), p. 44.
Review praises film as "technically expert," but objects that it doesn't "add up to" anything. Reprinted in No. 332.

197 Crowther, Bosley. "They Bite—But Can They Chew?" *New York Times* (20 November), II, p. 1.
Argument against giving directors too much freedom sees *Cul-De-Sac* as "overblown" with no "logic or purpose."

198 Delahaye, Michel, and Fieschi, Jean-André. "Landscape of a Mind: Interview with Roman Polanski." *Cahiers du Cinéma in English*, no. 3 (February), pp. 28–35.
Translation of No. 199. Reprinted in No. 552.

199 Delahaye, Michel, and Fieschi, Jean-André. "Paysage d'un Cerveau." *Cahiers du Cinéma*, no. 175 (February), pp. 44–51.
An interview in which Polanski talks about his schooling in Poland, his reasons for filming outside his native country, his desire to work with his own script, and the making of *Repulsion* and *Knife in the Water*. Translated in No. 198.

200 Delmas, Jean. "Cinéma Différent." *Jeune Cinéma*, no. 11 (January), p. 35.
Very brief review of *When Angels Fall*.

201 Delmas, Jean. *"Cul-De-Sac."* *Jeune Cinéma*, no. 19 (December), pp. 35–36.
Cul-De-Sac presents "unexpected" solutions to equally unexpected situations; Polanski is compared to the entomologist who puts three strange insects into the same bottle and then observes, with an attentive and slightly wicked eye, the "contortions of their battles" over dominance or submission.

*202 Dherbecourt, Dominique. *"Répulsion."* *Jeune Cinéma*, no. 12 (February).
Cited in Belmans. *See* No. 346.

203 Durgnat, Raymond. *"Cul-De-Sac."* *Films and Filming*, 12, no. 10 (July), 18, 51–52.

Film is reviewed as it relates to American and French generic traditions as well as Absurdism, Surrealism and Polish Romanticism. Though it "recalls Bunuel," it remains lightweight because of its "reliance on melo-drama and parody."

204 Ellison, Harlan. "Three Faces of Fear." *Cinema* [Los Angeles], 3, no. 2 (March), 13–14.
A consideration of Val Lewton's achievement in horror films includes an analysis of *Repulsion*, calling it "the closest thing to a perfect film of fear we have had since Lewton." But Polanski has failed to provide adequate answers to questions of "motive and personality" in the film. Illustrated.

205 Fieschi, Jean-André. "*Cul-De-Sac.*" *Cahiers du Cinéma*, no. 183 (October), p. 29.
Very brief review of *Cul-De-Sac*.

206 French, Philip. "Deadly Games For Three." *The Observer* (5 June), p. 24.
Review of *Cul-De-Sac* focuses on Polanski's skill and economy in pre-senting an allegorical black comedy which is "compellingly presented, with a personal, obsessive undercurrent."

207 Gill, Brendan. "Dead End." *The New Yorker*, 42 (12 November), 115.
Reviewer traces Polanski's "lessening of conviction" in dealing with basic human emotions from the exciting *Knife in the Water* to *Cul-De-Sac*, the "quintessence of fashionable, phony movie-making."

208 Gregor, Ulrich. "Berlin." *Cinéma 66* [Paris], no. 109, p. 123.
Brief review of *Cul-De-Sac* considers it as a return to Polanski's concerns in his early Polish films, citing the director's ability to mix comedy with horror and his polemicism.

209 Hartung, Philip. "Slick and Sick." *Commonweal*, 85 (25 November), 230.
Cul-De-Sac is a "handsomely made" and well-directed black comedy which alternates scenes of "realistic humor and grim brutality." Although Polanski's enigmatic meaning "can be annoying," his film effectively portrays the world's madness.

210 Haudiquet, Philippe. "*Répulsion.*" *Image et Son*, no. 192 (March), p. 110.
Review praises Polanski's "realistic" handling of psychological derange-ment, but objects to his excessive emphasis on cruelty. Illustrated.

211 Kahan, Saul. "Transylvania, Polanski Style." *Cinema* [Los Angeles], 3, no. 3 (December), 7–9.
Brief photo-essay on the making of *The Fearless Vampire Killers* with quotes from Polanski.

212 Kauffmann, Stanley. "*Knife in the Water*" in his *A World on Film*. New York: Harper, pp. 358–60.
Reprint of No. 104.

213 Kyrou, Ado. *Amour-Érotisme et Cinéma.* Edited by Eric Losfeld. Paris: Le Terrain Vague, pp. 64, 133, 166.
Author mentions "surreal" short films, and *Repulsion.*

214 Lajeunesse, Jacqueline. *"Répulsion." Image et Son: La Saison Cinématographique,* nos. 190/191 (January-February), pp. 221–22.
Brief review objects that film interests us in Carol's illness but does not involve us in it. Illustrated.

215 MacDonald, Dwight. *"Repulsion." Esquire,* 65 (April), 60, 62.
Although the reviewer finds the first hour of the film "brilliant, fluent, inventive and beautifully controlled," he feels that Polanski's detachment from the material and the "eccentricity" of his theme result in a tedious, over-played final half.

216 Martin, Marcel. "Pour Reparler de *Répulsion." Cinéma 66* [Paris], no. 104, pp. 122–23.
Response to article by Claire Clouzot (No. 193) argues that "clinical exactness" in the portrayal of Carol is unnecessary and that the details used to express her madness have "extraordinary dramatic force."

217 M[aslin], J[anet]. "Absurdity Kit." *Newsweek,* 68 (21 November), 129–30.
In *Cul-De-Sac,* Polanski plays "games" with answers known only to himself, "poses and prattles" with some "pleasant slapstick."

218 Milne, Tom. *"Cul-De-Sac." Sight and Sound,* 35, no. 3 (Summer), 146–47.
Review compares film to Pinter while listing typical Polanskian elements: "a ghoulish black comedy; the pain of solitude; pride; a touch of masochism; and above all, people and objects at odds with a landscape." Illustrated.

*219 Pérez, Michel. *"Cul-De-Sac." Combat* (9 July).
Cited in Belmans. *See* No. 346.

220 Picaper, Jean-Paul. "Au Festival De Berlin." *Le Monde* (7 July), p. 12.
Article reports the awarding of the Golden Bear of the Berlin Festival to *Cul-De-Sac,* a film concerning the impossibility of men understanding each other, in spite of their interdependence.

221 Powell, Dilys. "Trio In A Nightmare." *The Sunday Times* (5 June), p. 25.
Review discusses the twisted tensions of *Cul-De-Sac* as repetitive of those explored in *Knife in the Water* carried to an extreme: "an essay in the psychopathic" . . . "a claustrophobic nightmare, too well done to let you get away."

222 Salachas, Gilbert et al. *"Répulsion." Téléciné,* no. 127 (January-February), pp. 50–51.
Review praises film's union of psychology and Surrealism, which sets it apart from other horror films. Followed by brief comments from several other critics.

223 Sarris, Andrew. *"Cul-De-Sac, Georgy Girl."* *Village Voice*, 12, no. 7 (1 December), 27.

In the context of the review of *Cul-De-Sac*, which was suddenly pulled out of its theatrical run after unfavorable reviews, Sarris discusses the market and pressures besetting the "art" film. Discussion of the film centers on its Absurdist origins and Polanski's determination "to outrage his audience at all costs."

224 Schickel, Richard. "The Witless Urge To Be Too Funny." *Life*, 61 (9 December), 19.

Cul-De-Sac represents a rather "perfectly decent little movie idea" destroyed by the trend in the movie industry to reduce every filmic statement to a bad joke, in this case black humor. Polanski "oversells" his point with tasteless sensationalism and so loses what might have been "a satisfyingly sad commentary on mistaken ambitions."

225 Troszczyński, Jerzy. "Miedzy Londynem i Hollywoodem." *Film*, no. 46, 12–13.

Polanski discusses film-making in Hollywood and the restrictions on a director's work in this commercial system. Illustrated.

226 Vitoux, Frédéric. *"Répulsion."* *Midi-Minuit Fantastique*, no. 14 (June), pp. 111–15.

In *Repulsion*, Polanski "enriches the unreal, the immediate fantasy" of this film with the realism of his short films. However, the inclusion of both views results in the film's originality and its limitations.

227 Weiler, A. H. "Vivien Faces East." *New York Times* (6 November), II, pp. 13, 19.

Report of Polanski's current movie-making activities: *Cherchez La Femme* and a Western entitled *Half Breed*.

*228 d'Yvoire, Jean. *"Répulsion."* *Télérama*, no. 836 (23–29 January).
Cited in Belmans. *See* No. 346.

1967

229 Anon. "Blood on the Soapsuds." *Time*, 90 (24 November), 90.
Although review notes Polanski's wish to disassociate himself from *The Fearless Vampire Killers* because of U. S. cuts, "too many connections" involve him in a film "neither spooky nor spoofy." Illustrated.

230 Anon. *"Cul-De-Sac."* *Filmfacts*, 9, no. 23 (1 January), 319–20.
Brief plot synopsis with excerpts from reviews in *Time*, *New York Times*, *The New York World-Journal-Tribune*, *Saturday Review*, and *Variety*. Illustrated.

231 Anon. "Roman Polanski." *International Film Guide*. Edited by Peter Cowie. London: Tantivy and New York: A. S. Barnes, pp. 22–26.
Consideration of director's life and career praises his "ability to trap emotions in his imagery and not merely through his dialogue" and identifies the common theme of his work as "the struggle for supremacy

in a hostile and indifferent world." Polanski's interest in exploring "the labyrinths of human perversion" is likened to Franju. His work makes "the normal ... appear suddenly ambivalent and the strange ... seem deceptively reasonable." Illustrated.

232 Anon. "Vampire killers in limbo." *The Times* [London] (27 July), p. 8.
Brief news story outlines Polanski's problems with Martin Ransohoff over the editing of *Fearless Vampire Killers.*

233 Beau. *"The Beautiful Swindlers."* *Variety* (1 November), p. 7.
Polanski's episode has "a superficially jazzy look that ill conceals its flabby content."

234 Butler, Ivan. "Polanski and *Repulsion.*" *The Horror Film.* International Film Guide Series, London: A. Zivemmer and New York: A. S. Barnes, pp. 111–22.
Discussion focuses on how the director "invites us to share, and thus to understand, Carol's repulsion" through the manipulation of visual and aural imagery and point of view. Illustrated. Reprinted in No. 330.

235 Crowther, Bosley. *"The Fearless Vampire Killers or Pardon Me, But Your Teeth Are in My Neck."* *New York Times* (14 November), p. 52.
Review praises film as "superbly scenic and excitingly photographed," but sees its spoof of horror movies as "dismal." Reprinted in No. 333.

*236 Eberhardt, Konrad. " 'Horror' Codzienności." *Film,* no. 27, p. 5.
Cited by Filmoteka Polska; See No. 681. Illustrated.

*237 Fuksiewicz, Jacek. *"Repulsion."* *Kultura,* no. 28, p. 11.
Cited by Filmoteka Polska; See No. 681.

*238 Grzelecki, Stanislaw. *"Cul-De-Sac."* *Życie Warszawy,* no. 166, p. 8.
Cited by Filmoteka Polska; See No. 681.

*239 Grzelecki, Stanislaw. *"Repulsion."* *Życie Warszawy,* no. 166, p. 4.
Cited by Filmoteka Polska; See No. 681.

*240 Guze, Joanna. "Parabole Polańskiego." *Film,* no. 32, p. 4.
Cited by Filmoteka Polska; See No. 681. Illustrated.

*241 Hamilton, Jack. *"Repulsion."* *Kultura,* no. 27, p. 12.
Cited by Filmoteka Polska; See No. 681.

*242 Hellen, Tomasz. *"Cul-De-Sac."* *Pomorze,* no. 16, p. 16.
Cited by Filmoteka Polska; See No. 681.

*243 Jackiewicz, Aleksander. *"Cul-De-Sac."* *Życie Literackie,* no. 31, p. 5.
Cited by Filmoteka Polska; See No. 681.

*244 Jackiewicz, Aleksander. "Polański." *Życie Warszawy,* no. 263, p. 6.
Cited by Filmoteka Polska; See No. 681. Illustrated.

*245 J. J. S. "Repulsion." Tygodnik Powszechny, no. 52, p. 9.
Cited by Filmoteka Polska; See No. 681.

*246 Kakolewski, Krzysztof. "Polański Jako Moralista." Film, no. 33, p. 6.
Cited by Filmoteka Polska; See No. 681. Illustrated.

*247 Kalużyński, Zygmunt. "Cul-De-Sac." Polityka, no. 32, p. 12.
Cited by Filmoteka Polska; See No. 681. Illustrated.

*248 Kalużyński, Zygmunt "Repulsion." Polityka, no. 28, p. 12.
Cited by Filmoteka Polska; See No. 681. Illustrated.

*249 Kochański, Kazimierz. "Repulsion." Tygodnik Kulturalny, no. 28,
p. 12.
Cited by Filmoteka Polska; See No. 681. Illustrated.

*250 Lerman, L. "International Movie Report." Mademoiselle, 64 (Febru-
ary), 119.
Cited in Schuster, Mel. Motion Picture Directors. Metuchen, N.J.: The
Scarecrow Press, 1973, 300.

*251 Marszalek, Rafal. "Polański: Samotnosć, Slabość, Niewola." Dialog,
no. 9, pp. 136–40.
Cited by Filmoteka Polska; See No. 681.

252 Morgenstern, Joseph. "Bite and Tell." Newsweek, 70 (27 November), 98.
Brief review calls The Fearless Vampire Killers a "television-skittish spoof"
that is "child's play compared with the real thing." Illustrated.

*253 Nodzyński, Wieslaw. "Cul-De-Sac." Nadodrze, no. 18, p. 5.
Cited by Filmoteka Polska; See No. 681. Illustrated.

254 Sheed, Wilfred. "Films." Esquire, 67 (March), 20–21.
Cul-De-Sac depicts the "parody of a love-triangle movie, in which all
the emotions are inverted and all the connections are missing"; although
not based on a very good script and heavy-handed in its black humor,
Polanski's "knack for the sinister" seems to contain a powerful secret.

*255 Tatarkiewicz, Anna. "Cul-De-Sac." Polityka, no. 9, p. 8.
Cited by Filmoteka Polska; See No. 681.

*256 Terlecki, Wladyslaw. "Repulsion." Współczesność, no. 17, p. 3.
Cited by Filmoteka Polska; See No. 681.

257 Yorke, Gabriel. "The Slavic Odyssey of Roman Polanski." The
Village Voice (18 May), pp. 27–30.
Article covers biographical background and years at Lodz film school.

*258 Zaremba, Janusz. "Bardzo Zabawny Film. 'Matnia.'" Ekran, no. 31,
p. 6.
Cited by Filmoteka Polska; See No. 681. Illustrated.

1968

259   Adler, Renata. "*Rosemary's Baby.*" *New York Times* (13 June), p. 57.
Review praises Polanski's success in portraying paranoid fantasies as
making "absolute sense," but objects that the film is "not very scary."
Illustrated. Reprinted in No. 327.

260   Alpert, Hollis. "War and Witches." *Saturday Review*, 51 (15 June), 49.
Rosemary's Baby represents "a splendidly executed example of its genre,"
stylishly effective and convincing in execution of mood and performance.

261   Anon. "*Cul-De-Sac.*" *Film Comment*, 5, no. 1 (Fall), 4–9.
See No. 278.

*262   Anon. "*Fearless Vampire Killers.*" *Senior Scholastic*, 91 (11 Janu-
ary), 19.
Cited in Limerick, Zada, ed. *Readers' Guide to Periodical Literature*.
Vol. 28. New York: H. W. Wilson Company, 1968, 780.

263   Anon. "Polanski Biography, Filmography." *Film Comment*, 5, no. 1
(Fall), 10.
Biography, filmography following interview. *See* No. 278.

264   Anon. "Polanski: 'Truffaut, Lelouch, Godard: Little Kids Playing
at Revolution.'" *Variety* (12 June), p. 3.
News story documents Polanski's disagreement with French New Wave
directors who protested the Cannes Film Festival.

265   Anon. "*Rosemary's Baby.*" *Filmfacts*, 11, no. 12 (15 July), 175–77.
Brief plot synopsis with excerpts from reviews in *Time, New York, New
York Times, Variety*, and *Saturday Review*. Illustrated.

266   Anon. "*Rosemary's Baby.*" *Time*, 91 (21 June), 84.
Brief review finds the film "superb suspense" especially in the surprisingly
"very real" acting abilities of Mia Farrow. Illustrated.

267   Anon. "*Rosemary's Baby* Given a 'C' Rating By Catholic Office."
New York Times (21 June), p. 45.
Brief news story.

268   Anon. "*The Dance of the Vampires.*" *International Film Guide*,
edited by Peter Cowie, vol. 5. London: Tantivy and New York: A. S.
Barnes, p. 85.
Brief review says film "bears its subject both respect and affection."

269   Anon. "*The Fearless Vampire Killers.*" *Filmfacts* (1 January),
pp. 355–56.
Brief plot synopsis and excerpts from reviews in *Saturday Review, New
York Times, Variety*, and *Time*. Illustrated.

270   Bean, Robin. "Adventures of Yurek." *Films and Filming*, 15, no. 3
(December), 58–60
Scriptwriter on *Knife in the Water* discusses career, working methods,
and collaboration with Polanski.

271 Brion, Patrick. "Filmographie de Polanski." *Cahiers du Cinéma,* no. 208 (January), p. 36.
Brief biography, and filmography through *Rosemary's Baby.*

272 Comolli, Jean-Louis. "Folie et Autres Rêves." *Cahiers du Cinéma,* no. 208 (January), pp. 32–35.
Polanski's films, although often mixing genres and often crossing genre lines, do contain a certain unifying thread in their "fundamental inversion: madness is the most frightening thing, and sorcerers are preferable to it."

273 Corliss, Richard. "Film Chronicle." *National Review,* 20 (24 September), 969.
Although often "sloppily directed," *Rosemary's Baby* fascinates as a good ghost story on the strength of Mia Farrow's performance.

274 Crist, Judith. "Idle Dreams About Idols," in her *The Private Eye, the Cowboy and the Very Naked Girl.* New York: Holt, Rinehart and Winston, 194–97.
Reprint of No. 195.

275 Delahaye, Michel, and Narboni, Jean. "Entretien avec Roman Polanski." *Cahiers du Cinéma,* no. 208 (January), pp. 22–31.
Interview concerns background and conceptual matters relating to *The Fearless Vampire Killers* primarily, which the authors consider Polanski's most important film to date; also contains discussion of *Rosemary's Baby* and Polanski's views on fear and madness.

276 Delahaye, Michel. "*Le Bal des Vampires.*" *Cahiers du Cinéma,* no. 200/201 (April-May), pp. 119–20.
Polanski's *Fearless Vampire Killers* is at once "a great experimental film, a great adventure film, and a great comedy" containing "startling" stylistic qualities.

277 Ellison, Harlan. "*Rosemary's Baby.*" *Cinema* [Los Angeles], 4, no. 3 (Fall), 41–42.
Rosemary's Baby is a "classic" among fantasy films, because it makes "old horrors" relevant for our times. The acting is outstanding, as is the script, which balances a "story of suspense" with a "study of [a] young girl going psychopathically paranoid." Illustrated.

278 Engle, Harrison. "Polanski in New York." *Film Comment,* 5, no. 1 (Fall), 4–9.
Question-and-answer interview with Polanski focuses on his working methods and visual aesthetics. Contains reprints of reviews of *Rosemary's Baby* and a brief news item from *Variety.* Illustrated.

279 Gilliatt, Penelope. "The Chaos of Cool." *The New Yorker,* 44 (15 June), 87–89.
As a "horror film about pregnancy," *Rosemary's Baby* is elegantly executed and photographed, but ultimately fails to frighten because it lacks "the chill, common daylight of good thrillers." Reprinted in No. 407.

280 Hamilton, Jack. "From Best Seller to Movie Chiller." *Life*, 32 (25 June), 91–94.

Photo-story on the filming of *Rosemary's Baby* discusses Polanski's ("the little giant") working methods, demands on actors, and fascination for the macabre which "shocks bourgeois audiences who cannot accept that other people may be different from them." Illustrated.

281 Hart, Henry. "*Rosemary's Baby.*" *Films in Review*, 19, no. 7 (August–September), 456–57.

Very brief review criticizes confusion in Polanski's script and direction of a film dealing with "merely an elucidation of pregnancy-insanity."

282 Hartung, Philip. "*Rosemary's Baby.*" *Commonweal*, 88 (14 June), 384–85.

Slow pace of opening half of *Rosemary's Baby* contains the carefully crafted bits of information and detail necessary for the shocks in its suspenseful climax which "will make your blood run cold."

283 Hatch, Robert. "Films." *Nation*, 207 (22 July), 60–61.

Rosemary's Baby proves a "chic disappointment" in its slow development and lack of mystery.

284 Kauffmann, Stanley. "Son of a Witch." *The New Republic*, 158 (15 June), 26.

Review calls film "merely entertaining" (contrasting it with the "fine" *Knife in the Water*), but establishes Polanski as a "manufacturer of intelligent thrillers, clever and insubstantial." Reprinted in No. 355.

285 Mollet, Guy, and Thirard, Paul-Louis. "*Le Bal des Vampires.*" *Positif*, no. 94 (April), pp. 59–61.

Two commentaries on *Fearless Vampire Killers* discuss Polanski's film as a Dadaist equation of opposites, and as an "honorable failure" because it fails against standards of his earlier works.

286 Myers, Fred. "Shivery Conundrum." *Christian Century*, 85 (18 September), 1177.

Rosemary's Baby fails to be suspenseful for those who have read the novel as Polanski follows the book "too closely"; although performances are excellent and the film well crafted, the final scene "fails to satisfy."

287 Pearson, Maisie K. "*Rosemary's Baby*: The Horns of a Dilemma." *Journal of Popular Culture*, 2, no. 3 (Winter), 493–501.

Discussion of Ira Levin's novel as an opposition between modern "relative" values and older "absolute" ones refers to Polanski's film, which "closely follows" the book.

288 Sarris, Andrew. "Roman Polanski," in his *The American Cinema*. New York: Dutton, 151.

Sarris includes Polanski in his list of "Fringe Benefits"; a "genuinely unpredictable" director whose "talent is as undeniable as his intentions are dubious."

289 Sarris, Andrew. "*Rosemary's Baby.*" *The Village Voice*, 13, no. 41 (25 July), 37.

Review sees film as the result of a fortunate blending of the talents of Polanski and Ira Levin, "Levin being more of a story teller than a stylist and Polanski more a stylist than a story teller." The film deals obliquely with two fears, "the fear of pregnancy, . . . and the fear of a deformed offspring." Reprinted in No. 341.

290 Sheed, Wilfrid. "Films." *Esquire*, 70 (November), 26–28.

Very brief review finds *Rosemary's Baby* "passable," but lacking suspense as a result of Ruth Gordon's "rasping performance."

291 Simon, John. "Unanswerable Films, Answerable Letters." *The New Leader*, 51, no. 14 (8 July), 22–23.

Rosemary's Baby is cited as proof that "Polanski likes to make trashy films." Reprinted in No. 359.

292 Taylor, John Russell. "A horrible week." *The Times* [London] (5 December), p. 17.

Very brief review dismisses *Fearless Vampire Killers* as a "barren waste."

293 Walsh, Moira. "*Rosemary's Baby.*" *America*, 119 (20 July), 51–52.

Review criticizes the National Catholic Office of Motion Pictures' condemned rating of *Rosemary's Baby* for its "rigid and unpersuasive terms" and calls for informed critical leadership in educating the public about films.

294 Houston, Beverle, and Kinder, Marsha. "*Rosemary's Baby.*" *Sight and Sound*, 38, no. 1 (Winter), 17–26.

Polanski's film uses visual devices to create a "conflict of perception" to force us to accept Satanism as "an undeniable reality, however bizarre." This effect is achieved by presenting a "complex and textured surface" that gives rise to "visual conflict," and the feeling of conflict is echoed by the acting, which expresses "three modes of reality," as well as by the movie's "competing mythologies." These conflicts force us to question the way we "assign beliefs to our myths"; and how these beliefs relate to "reality." Illustrated.

295 McArthur, Colin. "Polanski." *Sight and Sound*, 38, no. 1 (Winter), 14–17.

Polanski's roots in the Polish Avant-Garde are considered, especially the ties to Surrealism and the Theater of the Absurd. His work is unique, however, by virtue of the theme of sexuality explored by all his films. Illustrated.

296 Ross, T. J. "Roman Polanski, *Repulsion*, and the New Mythology." *Film Heritage*, 4, no. 2 (Winter), 1–10.

By comparing Catherine Deneuve to the youth in *Knife in the Water* and the owner of the castle in *Cul-De-Sac*, we see that she is like a poet whose "affecting power" reveals the "passionlessness of the mundane." Her psychosis "puts her at an angle to the everyday scene which is close to that of a poet's," and what drives her mad is "what exacerbates and drives a poet to creation." Illustrated. Reprinted in No. 386.

297 Shivas, Mark. "*Rosemary's Baby.*" *Movie*, no. 16 (Winter), p. 39.
Very brief review considers the film brilliantly done as long as it retains
its "ambiguity of appearances."

1969

298 Anon. "Hollywood Murders." *Newsweek*, 74 (18 August), 28.
Brief description of discovery of murder scene. Illustrated.

299 Anon. "Night of Horror." *Time*, 94 (22 August), 16–17.
Article presents background details on lives of victims of Tate murders.
Illustrated.

300 Anon. "Nothing but bodies." *Time*, 94 (15 August), 24.
Brief account of discovery of murder scene at Polanski's home. Illustrated.

301 Anon. "Polanski denies orgy and drug stories." *The Times* [London]
(20 August), p. 4.
News story of interview with Polanski following his wife's death. Illustrated.

302 Anon. "Polanski, Roman." *Current Biography*, 30 (June), 39.
Biographical sketch contains a few minor inaccuracies. Illustrated. Reprinted in No. 303.

303 Anon. "Polanski, Roman," in *Current Biography Yearbook*. Edited
by Charles Moritz. New York: H. W. Wilson Company, 347–49.
Reprint of No. 302, with some revisions. Illustrated.

304 Anon. "*Rosemary's Baby* Censored in London." *New York Times*
(14 January), p. 35.
Brief news story quotes Polanski's condemnatory remarks about censorship
of his film for reasons of "kinky sex."

305 Anon. "Tate set." *Newsweek*, 74 (25 August), 24–25.
Report on police investigation into murders.

306 Anon. "*The Beautiful Swindlers.*" *Filmfacts*, 11, no. 24 (15 January), 530–31.
Brief plot synopsis and excerpts from review in *Variety*.

307 Anon. "The Times Diary." *The Times* [London] (15 January), p. 8.
News story quotes Polanski's reaction to British censors' cutting of
Rosemary's Baby.

308 Bradbury, Ray. "A New Ending to *Rosemary's Baby.*" *Films and
Filming*, 15, no. 11 (August), 10.
Bradbury objects to film's ending on grounds of psychological and tonal
consistency, and suggests an alternative one in which Rosemary steals
her baby back from the Satanists and seeks shelter with it in a church.
Reprinted in No. 376.

309 Chappetta, Robert. "*Rosemary's Baby.*" *Film Quarterly*, 22, no. 3
(Spring), 35–38.

Polanski's talent "for the baroque" gives way to "visual blandness," and his technique "of contrasting the bizarre with the bland" is "crude and forced." The movie's ending, however, works on the level of parody, though most audiences fail to see it in this way.

310 Ciment, Michel, Pérez, Michel, and Tailleur, Roger. "Entretien Avec Roman Polanski." *Positif*, no. 102 (February), pp. 6–19.
Polanski primarily discusses *Rosemary's Baby*, his adaptation of the novel, general approach to the filming, and public reaction, as well as other films within the context of his current filmmaking concerns and attitudes.

311 Corliss, Richard. "Still Legion, Still Decent?" *Commonweal*, 90, no. 10 (23 May), 289–92.
Rosemary's Baby represents a test case for the power of the "C" (Condemned) rating of the National Catholic Office for Motion Pictures which wishes to limit today's "lax screen morals" while remaining relevant to film as an art form. History of the NCOMP and the MPAA concludes with Polanski's "moral" treatment of his material in the film which, in its popularity, demonstrated that the NCOMP no longer has the power to prohibit a film.

312 Gow, Gordon. *"Rosemary's Baby." Films and Filming*, 15, no. 6 (March), 38–39.
Review praises Polanski's visual style and Mia Farrow's performance but criticizes editing and casting of Ruth Gordon. Polanski has "used colour for mood very well," but "shocks are absent." Illustrated.

313 Gow, Gordon. "Satisfaction: A Most Unpleasant Feeling." *Films and Filming*, 15, no. 7 (April), 15–19.
Polanski talks about his life and art, including his distaste for movie endings that "satisfy" an audience. His remarks are placed in the context of a critical biographical essay that sees Polanski's work as focusing on "disoriented individuals in conflict with a hostile, or seemingly hostile, society." The director's future projects and his use of long takes are also discussed at length. Illustrated.

314 Grzelecki, Stanislaw. *Twenty Years of Polish Cinema*. Warsaw: Art and Film Publishers.
Introduction on "Polish Feature Film, 1947-1967" mentions the "brilliant direction" of *Knife in the Water*; body of book contains stills with captions from films of these years.

315 Hibbin, Nina. *Eastern Europe*. New York: A. S. Barnes, 107–108.
Brief biography and filmography. Illustrated.

316 Kernan, Margot. *"Rosemary's Baby." International Film Guide*, edited by Peter Cowie, vol. 6. London: Tantivy and New York: A. S. Barnes, 173–74.
Brief review sees film as "entertaining" and comments on the director's "observant" casting, "keen eye for American patterns," and "fascination with the symbolic qualities of architecture and . . . affinity for inner space." Illustrated.

317 McCarty, John Alan. "The Polanski Puzzle." *Take One*, 2, no. 5 (May-June), 18–21.
All Polanski's films contain the "theme of isolation, wherein the protagonist or antagonist's private world is intruded upon by strangers, a situation which always ends in some form of violence, self-destruction, or disaster." Most focus on the relationship between fear and sex, and are concerned with presenting the effects of neuroses by showing us "surreal worlds." The settings are "the chief antagonists." Illustrated.

318 Mayersberg, Paul. "Polanski's Atmosphere." *New Society*, 13 (30 January), 175.
The director's career is discussed in terms of the way he deals with "fear of the unknown" through the subjects he chooses and through his creation of atmosphere. Illustrated.

319 Nairn, Tom. "Roman Polanski." *Cinema* [Cambridge], no. 3 (June), pp. 22–26.
Polanski's strength lies in his "exceptional talent for social satire," expressed through "humorous grotesques" in a Surrealist assault upon the audience, rather than in his "relatively weak attempts at the horror game."

320 Pérez, Michel. "La Petite Accouchée de L'Amerique (*Rosemary's Baby*)." *Positif*, no. 102 (February), pp. 1–5.
Perez notes that, contrary to what would be expected, Polanski chose to film *Rosemary's Baby* with "a maximum of realist precision"; in this manner Polanski shows great fidelity in his adaptation of Ira Levin's book. The stunning contrast between the bourgeois, quotidian life of Rosemary and the apparent mystical sorcerism of her neighbors throws the "real world" into question: even "the least package of Pall Malls appears to us ambiguous." However, Perez says, "it is clear that the devil and sorcery hardly excite Polanski . . . *Rosemary's Baby* appears as a brilliant stylistic exercise appropriate to seduce a young filmmaker desirous of proving himself before the Hollywood machine. . . ."

321 Polanski, Roman. "Satisfaction—A Most Pleasant Feeling." *Films and Filming*, 15, no. 7 (April), 15–19.
Inaccurate citation of No. 313 listed in MacCann, Richard Dyer and Edward S. Perry. *The New Film Index*. New York: E. P. Dutton & Co., 1975, 303.

322 Reisner, Joel, and Kane, Bruce. "An Interview with Roman Polanski." *Cinema* [Los Angeles], 5, no. 2, 11–15.
Polanski discusses his influences and his methods of working with actors, cameramen and musicians. All of the films are covered, and Polanski expresses opinions about free will, Freudian symbolism, the press, sex and violence in film.

323 Stewart, Bruce. "Excelsior: Roman Polanski." *The Month*, 41 (May), pp. 307–309.
Overview of Polanski's career sees films since *Knife in the Water* as containing a "worrying absence of purpose."

324 Tarratt, Margaret. *"Rosemary's Baby."* *Screen,* 10, no. 2 (March-April), 90–96.
Film is discussed as manifestation of "social evil" in America, an evil founded on "myths" and "superstition." Rosemary's "unsentimental innocence" separates her from the other characters and exposes her to the "horror concealed beneath the surface veneer of the habitual and the socially acceptable," which is rationalized by others with "glib psychoanalytic jargon."

325 Taylor, John Russell. "A glossy psychological thriller." *The Times* [London] (23 January), p. 7.
Review calls *Rosemary's Baby* Polanski's "most satisfying film" because it has "no noticeable pretensions." Illustrated.

326 Thompson, T. "Tragic Trip to the House on a Hill." *Life,* 67 (29 August), 42–46.
Article describes Polanski's revisit to murder scene, including biographical detail and background on his life and marriage. Illustrated.

1970

327 Adler, Renata. *"Rosemary's Baby."* *New York Times Film Reviews 1913–1968,* vol. 5. New York: New York Times and Arno Press, 3764.
Reprint of No. 259.

328 Anon. "Bunny bubble." *The Times* [London] (22 August), p. 10.
Announcement of Hugh Hefner's plans to finance Polanski's *Macbeth.*

329 Anon. "Polanski to give evidence." *The Times* [London] (9 July), p. 5.
Brief announcement of Polanski's role in the trial of his wife's murderers.

330 Butler, Ivan. "Polanski and *Repulsion.*" *Horror in the Cinema.* International Film Guide Series, London: A. Zwemmer and New York: A. S. Barnes, 131–43.
Reprint of No. 234.

331 Butler, Ivan. *The Cinema of Roman Polanski.* International Film Guide Series. New York: A. S. Barnes and London: A. Zwemmer.
Butler's critical study gives in-depth analysis of each of the films through *Rosemary's Baby,* focusing on the director's Surrealism, themes of sexuality, connections with the Theater of the Absurd, and concern with atmosphere. Includes detailed plot summaries of the films, a biographical sketch, and much material gathered from personal interviews with the director and people who worked with him. Illustrated.

332 Crowther, Bosley. *"Cul-De-Sac."* *New York Times Film Reviews 1913–1968,* vol. 5. New York: New York Times and Arno Press, 3644–45.
Reprint of No. 196.

333 Crowther, Bosley. *"The Fearless Vampire Killers or Pardon Me, But Your Teeth Are in My Neck."* *New York Times Film Reviews 1913–1968,* vol. 5. New York: New York Times and Arno Press, 3713–14.
Reprint of No. 235.

334 Crowther, Bosley. *"Knife in the Water." New York Times Film Reviews 1913–1968*, vol. 5. New York: New York Times and Arno Press, 3420–21.
Reprint of No. 93.

335 Crowther, Bosley. "Movie on Insanity By Pole Opens at N. Y. Theatre." *New York Times Film Reviews 1913–1968*, vol. 5, New York: New York Times and Arno Press, 3569.
Reprint of No. 147.

336 Gelmis, Joseph. "Roman Polanski," in his *The Film Director as Superstar*. Garden City, N. Y.: Doubleday, 139–55.
Question-and-answer interview focuses on Polanski's childhood experiences, education, use of sound, and method of working. The influences of Surrealism and the Theatre of the Absurd on his work are also discussed, and there are comments on the production and reception of each of the films, including the shorts. One of the most useful interviews available on the director. Illustrated.

337 Kané, Pascal. *Roman Polanski*. Paris: Les Editions du Cerf.
Sections concern Polanski's "oeuvre" in terms of genre (particularly "witchcraft") and recurring themes in Polanski's work ("a general scheme: an external world only seen, neutral and impersonal—and rendered frightening by this same impersonality—and an internal universe, extremely personal, bound to strange laws; an imaginary world, mixing reality and the fantastic . . ."). The series of oppositions within his films evolve into meaning. Also includes interpretations of individual films (operating at both the level of "spectacle" and intellectual interpretation), and definitions of a "little lexicon of Polanskian terms."

338 Manchel, Frank. *Terrors of the Screen*. Englewood Cliffs, N. J.: Prentice-Hall, 93–94.
Brief discussion of *Repulsion* and *Rosemary's Baby* calls Polanski "an expert on audience manipulation," and considers *Rosemary's Baby* the most "aesthetically pleasing" and controversial film of recent years.

339 Mosk[owitz, Gene]. *"Cinema Different 3." Variety* (8 April), p. 24.
Review describes packaging of Polanski's "la Rivière de Diamants" with two other short features by Paris distributor.

340 Sarris, Andrew. *"Repulsion; The Ipcress File; The Hours of Love,"* in his *Confessions of a Cultist*. Touchstone: Simon and Schuster, 208–10.
Reprint of No. 170.

341 Sarris, Andrew. *"Rosemary's Baby,"* in his *Confessions of a Cultist*. Touchstone: Simon and Schuster, 373–76.
Reprint of No. 289.

342 Weinberg, Herman. "Basic Drama Is Two," in his *Saint Cinema*. New York: Drama Book Specialists, 231–32.

A recapitulation of the controversy surrounding the Oedipal implications of *Knife in the Water*, repeating Polanski's description of the film as a "conflict . . . between two people."

1971

343 Anon. *"Macbeth* by Daylight." *Time*, 97 (25 January), 45.
News story on production of film includes quotes from Polanski about his efforts to achieve authenticity. Illustrated.

344 Anon. *"Macbeth." Filmfacts*, 14, no. 24, n. d., 730–32.
Plot synopsis and excerpts of reviews from *Newsweek, The Chicago Sun-Times*, and *The San Francisco Chronicle*.

345 Belmans, Jacques. *Roman Polanski*. Paris: Editions Seghers.
First section comprises an historical-critical perspective (Polanski's films "serve to exorcise old terrors" of his traumatic youth); a summary of his early student films at Lodz emphasizing elements which recur within later films; a summary of the final shorts and *Knife in the Water* focusing on his highly developed, individual cinematic technique; and finally an analysis of Polanski's features in light of his ability to "always find the proper (filmic) language for treating his subject, . . ." The second section contains an extract from *Cul-De-Sac* and various opinions and reviews concerning Polanski's work, and a bibliography difficult in its inaccuracies.

346 Butler, Ivan. *The Making of Feature Films: A Guide*. Baltimore, Maryland: Penguin, 81–84, 178.
Chapter on "The Director" includes brief interview with Polanski concerning his background, work in England, scripting, settings, and use of color in his films.

347 Cluny, Claude Michel. *"Le Bal Des Vampires." Dossiers du Cinéma: Cineastes I*. Edited by Jean-Louis Bory and Claude Michel Cluny. Tournai, Belgium: Casterman, 17–20.
Avoiding the flaws of *Rosemary's Baby* and *Cul-De-Sac, The Fearless Vampire Killers* "attains real perfection." It "is admirably constructed, with the precision of poetry and the indispensable realism of fantasy," as Cocteau's films are. As in all such films, setting is of paramount importance, and its humor arises from the inversion of values and the unnaturalism of the images.

348 Cluny, Claude Michel. "Roman Polanski." *Dossiers du Cinéma: Cineastes I*. Edited by Jean-Louis Bory and Claude Michel Cluny. Tournai, Belgium: Casterman, 205–208.
Discussion of Polanski's creation of a closed world that "traps" the viewer by its communication of the "strange and marvellous" through objects, by its juxtaposition of moods of "humor and fear, subtle irony and violence," and by its use of restricted settings.

349 DuBois, Larry. "Playboy Interview: Roman Polanski." *Playboy* (December), pp. 93–118, 126.
Long question-and-answer interview focuses on Polanski's attitudes toward women, politics, his early life, and the murder of his wife. Illustrated.

350 Durgnat, Raymond. *"The Fat and the Lean." Films and Filming,* 17, no. 8 (May), 96, 100.

Polanski has made "a cynical slapstick tragedy" that explores the "co-ordinates of dominance and submission." However, the film lacks "a certain depth of common experience," which makes it appear as the work of a "child prodigy" or an "eternal student."

351 Freud, Clement. "An Odyssey In Wales: Roman Polanski's *Macbeth*." *Show,* 2, no. 4 (June), 24–28.

Feature story on the film's production, including an account of a visit to the set and quotes from Kenneth Tynan on Polanski's precise methods of scriptwriting and on his consciousness about the direction of movement across the screen. Illustrated.

352 Gow, Gordon. *Suspense in the Cinema.* New York: Coronet, Paperback Library, 58–60.

Consideration of how tension is developed in *Knife in the Water* and *Cul-De-Sac* by the "contrast between environment and events." In *Knife in the Water,* the isolated setting aboard a boat gives rise to tensions "both psychological and social," while *Cul-De-Sac* "gives the lie to the misfit's notion of an idyllic retreat."

353 Greenspun, Roger. *"Macbeth." New York Times* (21 December), p. 51.

Review praises film as best version of Shakespeare's play because it focuses on "interpretation" of text rather than on mere mechanical reproduction. Reprinted in No. 408.

354 Heaven, Simon. *"Macbeth:* A Brief Filmography." *Theatre Quarterly,* 1 (July-September), 53.

Mentions Polanski version of *Macbeth* in filmography.

355 Kauffmann, Stanley. *"Rosemary's Baby,"* in his *Figures of Light.* New York: Harper & Row, 83–85.

Reprint of No. 284.

*356 Leslie, Ann. "Roman Polanski: With a Little Help from His Friends." *Nova* (May), pp. 55–57.

Cited in King, Betty, ed. *British Humanities Index,* 1971. London: The Library Association, 1972, 327.

357 Murf. [Murphy, Arthur D.] *"Macbeth." Variety* (15 December), pp. 14, 18.

Review praises film's "pervading virility."

358 Shivas, Mark. "They're Young, They're in Love, They're the Macbeths." *New York Times* (28 February), II, p. 13.

Story about the production of *Macbeth* contains quotes from Polanski and others about the youthfulness of Macbeth and Lady Macbeth. Illustrated.

359 Simon, John. "Declines and Pratfalls of Major Directors," in his *Movies Into Film.* New York: Delta, 181–82.

Reprint of No. 291.

360　Taylor, John Russell. "Skolimowski's baroque bath-house." *The Times* [London] (26 October), p. 12.
Review of *Deep-End* makes brief mention of critic's "unorthodox" views on Polanski.

361　Tynan, Kenneth. "Polish Imposition." *Esquire*, 76, no. 3 (September), 122–25.
Profile of Polanski focuses on his "imposing" personality and his "conservative" political ideas. Tynan's experiences while working with the director on *Macbeth* are also outlined. Reprinted in No. 362.

362　Tynan, Kenneth. "The Magnetic Pole." *Sunday London Times Magazine* (7 November), pp. 32–43.
Reprint of No. 361.

*363　Vronskaya, J. "Polanski's *Macbeth* and its antecedents." *Film*, 62 (Summer), 23.
Cited in Schuster, Mel. *Motion Picture Directors*. Metuchen, N.J.: The Scarecrow Press, 1973, 301.

364　Weintraub, Bernard. " 'If You Don't Show Violence the Way It Is,' Says Roman Polanski, 'I Think That's Harmful. If You Don't Upset People Then That's Obscenity.' " *New York Times Magazine* (12 December, VI, pp. 36–37, 64.
Long feature article contains biographical and critical survey and quotes from Polanski on violence, women and his career. Illustrated. Reprinted in *New York Times Biographical Edition* (12 December).

365　Whyte, Alistair. "Poland," in his *New Cinema in Eastern Europe*. London: Studio Vista; New York: Dutton, 44–48.
A consideration of Polanski as one of a "group of directors who broke away from the restrictions of socialist realism" focuses on his Polish-made films and notes two themes: the outsider in a thoughtlessly brutal society, and "the conflict of individuals thrown into a dependent relationship." Illustrated.

366　Wyndham, Francis. "The Young Macbeth." *Sunday London Times Magazine* (28 February), pp. 14, 19.
Report on the placement of Polanski's Macbeths within the two hundred year history of the roles, followed by an interview in which Polanski explains his "commonsense interpretation" of the play. Illustrated.

1972

367　Andrews, Nigel. "*Macbeth*." *Sight and Sound*, 41, no. 2 (Spring), 108.
Although the strength of Polanski's version lies in that it works simultaneously on a naturalistic and psychological plane, it lacks the "dynamic of a committed interpretation."

368　Anon. "Berlin award for Pasolini's Chaucer film." *The Times* [London] (5 July), p. 4.
Brief news story includes announcement of honorable mention given to *Weekend of a Champion* at The Berlin Festival.

*369 Anon. "British Cinema Filmography." *Film*, 65 (Spring), 10.
Cited in Schuster, Mel. *Motion Picture Directors*. Metuchen, N.J.: Scarecrow Press, 1973, 301.

370 Anon. "Landscapes of the Mind." *Time*, 99 (10 January), 59.
Very brief review of *Macbeth* concludes the film contains some interesting interpretive points and "gripping" visuals, but finally lacks the poetry and "force" of the play. Illustrated.

371 Anon. "*Macbeth* Is Voted Best Film By Board." *New York Times* (8 January), p. 19.
Brief news story tells of choice of *Macbeth* as best film of year by National Board of Review of Motion Pictures.

*372 Anon. "*Macbeth*." *Senior Scholastic*, 100 (14 February), 16–17.
Cited in Limerick, Zada, ed. *Readers' Guide to Periodical Literature*. Vol. 32. New York: H. W. Wilson Company, 1973, 785.

373 Anon. "The Making of *Macbeth*." *Playboy*, 19, no. 2 (February), 77–82.
Feature article on production of film includes history of screen versions of play and quotes from the director about his attempts to create a realistic mise-en-scène. Illustrated.

374 Anon. "What Directors Are Saying." *Action*, 7 (January-February), 37.
Brief excerpt from No. 373.

375 Belmans, Jacques. *Cinéma Et Violence*. Belgium: La Renaissance Du Livre, 41–44, 151.
Discussion of satire includes comments on Polanski's early short films primarily; "brief and stunning meditation on human cruelty and violence," concerns which continue into his features.

376 Bradbury, Ray. "A New Ending to *Rosemary's Baby*." *Focus on the Horror Film*. Edited by Roy Huss and T. J. Ross, Englewood Cliffs, N. J.: Prentice-Hall, 149–51.
Reprinted from No. 308.

377 Gow, Gordon. "*Macbeth*." *Films and Filming*, 18, no. 7 (April), 53–54.
Polanski's version of the play is not up to those of Kurasawa and Welles, but he leaves his "individual mark on it" while doing right by Shakespeare at the same time. Though the narrative "sags" in one or two places, the film "offers images of note." Polanski's use of violence and his decision to make the hero and heroine young are "true to the spirit of Shakespeare's play." Illustrated.

378 Hatch, Robert. "Films." *The Nation*, 214 (3 January), 28.
Polanski's *Macbeth* repeats other failures of filmed Shakespeare; the directors capture the melodrama but lose "his sense of high occasion" and thus produce a "visually expansive, morally reductive approach to Shakespeare."

379 Hawk. *"Weekend of a Champion." Variety* (12 July), p. 30.
Very brief review praises film produced by Polanski as "one of the best" of the genre portraying famous sports figures.

380 Houston, Penelope. "The Arts." *The Times* [London] (25 February), p. 11.
Brief review of *Weekend of a Champion* in which Polanski's "squirrel-like presence" is seen as a benefit.

381 Johnson, William. *"King Lear* and *Macbeth." Film Quarterly*, 25, no. 3 (Spring), 41–48.
Directors Peter Brook and Roman Polanski have both filmed versions of Shakespeare's plays that reflect Jan Kott's interpretation of the tragedies as Absurdist. By minimizing the characters' heroic stature, this orientation diminishes the playwright's "speculative vision." But Polanski ultimately escapes the restrictiveness of Kott's view when he "liberates Macbeth, letting him grow sufficiently larger than life to hold the film together."

382 Kael, Pauline. "Killers and Thieves." *The New Yorker*, 47 (5 February), 76.
Review draws parallels between *Macbeth* and the Manson murders, citing "slaughter" as the star of the film. The movie is a "simplification" of the play, and the youth of Macbeth and Lady Macbeth "diminishes our involvement." Reprinted in No. 411.

383 Kauffmann, Stanley. "On Film." *The New Republic*, 166 (1 January), 22, 32–33.
Review calls film a "straight, serious attempt" to adapt the play, though hampered by "inadequate" acting and a "slashed" text. Reprinted in No. 544.

384 Kydryński, Lucjan. "Kurier Warszawski." *Przekrój*, no. 1412 (30 April).
As of this article, Polanski considered *Macbeth* his best film to date. However, the author feels that, although the film presents good visuals and sense of horror, it lacks individuality and is ultimately boring.

385 Reilly, C[harles]. P[hillips]. *"Macbeth." Films in Review*, 23, no. 2 (February), 111–12.
Brief review criticizes casting of Macbeth and Polanski's "insensitive resort to excesses" in expansion of the play's preoccupation with blood. Illustrated.

386 Ross, T. J. "Polanski, *Repulsion*, and the New Mythology." *Focus on the Horror Film*. Edited by Roy Huss and T. J. Ross. Englewood Cliffs, N. J.: Prentice-Hall, 152–61.
Reprinted from No. 296.

387 Slojewski, Jan Zbigniew. *"Macbeth." Perspektywy*, no. 19, p. 31.
Review of *Macbeth* finds the film's violence unnecessary and inaccurate, and unlike Shakespeare's monumental style focuses upon the lives of "flies."

388 Strick, Philip. "Clubs." *Films and Filming*, 18, no. 7 (April), 81, 83.
Quotes from Polanski regarding his childhood experiences with the cinema, his method of writing screenplays, and his problems working with unions, followed by a review of *Macbeth*. In *Macbeth* "what matters is the subject," and "the importance of the script as the film's framework is observed so scrupulously that much of the film, one feels, could have been shot by anybody."

389 Strick, Philip. "*Macbeth.*" *Monthly Film Bulletin*, 39, no. 458 (March), 53.
Review sees film as successfully clearing up many of Shakespeare's "ambiguities" and notes its "sense of repeated intrusion and treachery."

390 Taylor, John Russell. "Polanski's success: keeping Shakespeare in his place." *The Times* [London] (4 February), p. 9.
Review sees *Macbeth* as most successful at the beginning and end, "faltering" in the middle with "long sustained scenes of Shakespeare's dialogue." Illustrated.

391 Wajda, Andrzej. "Reżyser filmowy i swiat współczesny. Andrzej Wajda w rozmowie z Romanem Polańskim." *Kino*, 7, no. 2 (February), 31–36.
Polanski praises the advantages of being cosmopolitan: one can more readily see the universal elements of various national traditions. He also speaks highly of the technical facilities available to him in the United States and argues that the pressures put on American directors by big business interests can be overcome by "muscle." He contrasts his feeling about Poland with that of Wajda, who was part of the War generation. For Polanski, the discovery of the Theater of the Absurd, which he found "very close to us [Poles]," was the crucial moment in his development as an artist. Translated in No. 558.

392 Young, Vernon. "*Knife in the Water,*" in his *On Film*. Chicago: Quadrangle, 366–68.
Review praises film as "an unveiled view of what men and women think they're about," in which all three characters are tested.

393 Young, Vernon. "Poetry, Politics, and Pornography," in his *On Film*. Chicago: Quadrangle, 307.
Footnote mentions Polanski's development as a "professional spook."

394 Zimmer, J. "*Macbeth.*" *Image et Son*, no. 262 (June-July), pp. 152–53.
Brief review praises Polanski's imaginative casting and attention to detail.

395 Zimmerman, Paul [D.]. "Man of Blood." *Newsweek*, 79 (10 January), 59.
Review links Polanski's obsession with violence, the excess in "unremitting horror," with the Manson murders.

1973

396 Allombert, G. "*Quoi?* (*What?*)" *Image et Son Revue du Cinéma*, nos. 276–277 (October), pp. 303–304.

Brief review praises Polanski's "savage humor" and calls the film "enchanting."

397 Alpert, Hollis. "No, No, Barbra." *Saturday Review/World*, 1 (6 November), 50.
Very brief review of *What?* considers it a "sneaky, dirty-minded little farce" that is "just plain awful."

398 Anon. "Best film actress award for Liza Minnelli." *The Times* [London] (1 March), p. 18.
Announcement of award to Anthony Mendleson for the costume design of *Macbeth* by the Society of Film and Television Arts.

399 Anon. "Polanski Ready for *China Town*." *New York Times* (9 September), p. 58.
Brief news story announces start of production on film.

400 Bartholomew, David. "*Macbeth*." *Cinefantastique*, 2, no. 2, 43–44.
Review praises Polanski's adaptation in following "Shakespeare's masterpiece with an unfailing skill and an unflinching camera" which results in an "uncommonly mature and forceful adaptation."

401 Berlin, Norman. "*Macbeth*: Polanski and Shakespeare." *Literature/Film Quarterly*, 1, no. 4 (Fall), 291–98.
Polanski has interpreted Shakespeare in a way that gives us "a view of life in our time." He views *Macbeth* from "the outside only, making the film more melodramatic than tragic," and he bathes the film in blood to show us "a world filled with confusions and madness . . . where tomorrows are as brutal as todays."

402 Canby, Vincent. "*What?*" *New York Times* (4 October), p. 57.
Review points out sexism and lack of purpose in film, but praises its beauty and sense of "anarchic comedy." Reprinted in No. 533.

403 Cluny, Claude Michel. "*Quoi? (What?)*." *Cinéma* 73, no. 175 (April), p. 153.
Brief review considers film as a failed comedy.

404 Codelli, Lorenzo. "*Quoi? (What?)*." *Positif*, no. 151 (June), p. 88.
Brief review claims that film provides "a vague phantom of the fascinating world of Polanski"; while he shows a fastidious concern with the movie's nonsensical surface, this surface covers "the most banal of realities." Illustrated.

405 Delmas, J[ean]. "*Quoi?*" *Jeune Cinéma*, no. 71 (June), pp. 41–43.
"Illogical and amoral as a dream," *What?* is cruel without being vulgar; however, its technical mastery is "too controlled" for a film whose "raison d'être" is freedom of the imagination.

406 Fuksiewicz, Jacek. *Polish Cinema*. Warsaw: Interpress Publishers, pp. 42–43, 56, 62.
Favorable but brief comments on Polanski's Polish-made shorts and *Knife in the Water*. Polanski's credits are not included in "Who's Who of Polish Film Makers" section. Illustrated.

407   Gilliatt, Penelope. "The Chaos of Cool," in her *Unholy Fools*. New York: Viking Press, pp. 104–106.
Reprint of No. 279.

408   Greenspun, Roger. *"Macbeth." New York Times Film Reviews 1971–1972*. New York: The New York Times and Arno Press, p. 194.
Reprint of No. 353.

°409   Hellen, Tomasz. "Macbeth." *Fakty 73*, no. 52, p. 11.
Cited by Filmoteka Polska; See No. 681. Illustrated.

410   Higham, Charles. "Polanski: *Rosemary's Baby* and After." *New York Times* (23 September), II, pp. 1, 13.
Interview with Polanski focuses on *Chinatown* scenario and influences of Absurdism and Surrealism.

411   Kael, Pauline. "Killers and Thieves," in her *Deeper Into Movies*. Boston and Toronto: Atlantic-Little, Brown, pp. 399–401.
Reprint of No. 382.

°412   Kałużyński, Zygmunt. "Macbeth." *Polityka*, no. 52, p. 10.
Cited by Filmoteka Polska; See No. 681.

413   Kauffmann, Stanley. "'Day for Night,' Two with MM." *The New Republic*, 169 (13 October), 36.
Very brief review of *What?* concludes that it contains the germ of an idea which never matured.

414   Lefèvre, Raymond. "*Quoi?*" *Image et Son Revue Du Cinéma*, no. 272 (May), pp. 119–20.
"Refusing all rational structure," Polanski has made a dream film in which he has allowed himself to be carried along by the easy fluidity of the creative impulse. Though the film is good-humore(, its end.ng is slightly bitter. As in fairy tales, the heroine's sexuality gives her "exorbitant power."

415   Leroux, A. "Macbeth." *Séquences*, no. 72 (April), pp. 31–33.
Reviewer defends violence in Polanski's *Macbeth* as an essential and main element of Shakespeare's play. However, in Polanski's fascination with the "exterior" violence, he has failed to develop the interior characterizations, thus the film's resulting imbalance.

416   McCarty, J. "Macbeth." *Cinefantastique*, 2, no. 3, 35.
Review praises superb film visuals and technical excellence which is in constant contention with the Shakespearian dialogue leaving its finest moments "pure Polanski" but ultimately "second-rate."

417   Mullin, Michael. "Macbeth on Film." *Literature/Film Quarterly*, 1, no. 4 (Fall), 332–42.
Comparison of various filmed adaptations of *Macbeth*. Polanski's version fails as an interpretation of Shakespeare because its realistic style gives us "the story behind the legend, seen from the viewpoint of history." Thus it remains "always outside the consciousness of its hero." Illustrated.

418 Reddington, John. "Film, Play and Idea." *Literature/Film Quarterly*, 1, no. 4 (Fall), 367–69.
Polanski's *Macbeth* fails as a valid interpretation of the play because of its "physical obdurateness" and because it retains none of Shakespeare's "living ambiguity." As a result, it is "merely Polanski" instead of Shakespeare.

419 Rothenbeucher, B. *"What?* Is Polanski Saying?" *Christian Century*, 90 (28 November), 1179–80.
Free from Hollywood commercial constraints, Polanski presents a film clearly reflecting his particular world view: 'ironic, subtle, strangely surreal-ambiguous"; a sensitive satire on today's decadence.

420 Rothwell, Kenneth S. "Roman Polanski's *Macbeth*: Golgotha Triumphant." *Literature/Film Quarterly*, 1, no. 1 (January), 71–75.
In Polanski's vision of the play, "violence is not merely gratuitous but the outward and visible sign for the King's, and mankind's, inner agony and suffering." But Polanski's decision to make Macbeth and his lady young "deprives us of a sense of pity and awe."

421 Sarris, Andrew. "Epiphanies from Truffaut." *The Village Voice*, 18 (11 October), 76.
Brief review calls *What?* Polanski's "least interesting and most exasperating film" because he has "failed to communicate any of its incidental pleasures in the form of humor, charm, or eroticism."

*422 Tatarkiewicz, Anna. *"Macbeth." Tygodnik Kulturalny*, nos. 52–53, 12.
Cited by Filmoteka Polska; *See* No. 681. Illustrated.

423 Warhol, Andy and Hackett, P. "Andy Warhol tapes Roman Polanski." *Interview*, no. 38 (November), pp. 6–13.
Rambling question-and-answer interview in which Polanski recounts some favorite stories about his life and his films. Illustrated.

424 Werb. [Werba, Hank]. *"Che?" Variety* (10 January), pp. 18, 30.
Review condemns film as "bits and pieces of erotica and black humor . . . bathed in excessive length."

425 Young, Vernon. "Fat Shakespeare, 'Fat City,' Lean Wilderness." *Hudson Review*, 26, no. 1 (Spring), 170–72.
Polanski's version of the "virtually unstageable" *Macbeth* stresses action to the detriment of Shakespeare's language, resulting in monotony of its blatant production "trading on the vogue for porno and spilled guts," according to the reviewer. Illustrated.

1974

*426 Ales, B. et al. "La violence est-elle plus nocive que la pornographie?" *Cine Revue*, 54 (24 January), 9–11.
Cited in Aceto, Vincent, Jane Graves and Fred Silva, eds. *Film Literature Index*. Vol. 2. New York and London: R. R. Bowker, 976, 382.

427 Alpert, H[ollis]. "Jack, The Private Eye." *Saturday Review/World*, 1 (27 July), 46.
Review examines the important role and influence of producer Robert Evans on the production of *Chinatown*, a film which is "clever, cunning, tricky, and superbly acted." Illustrated.

428 American Film Institute. *Dialogue on Film: Roman Polanski*, 3, no. 8 (August).
Polanski discusses his working methods and aesthetic preoccupations in an extensive, detailed question-and-answer interview. He emphasizes his difficulties with Robert Towne on *Chinatown*: ("I could not have *enough* interest in the visual side."). Also discussed is his predilection to set up a scene with actors before considering camera angles and his reactions to various cameramen and producers he has collaborated with. (Martin Ransohoff is severely criticized for re-cutting *Fearless Vampire Killers*.) He explains his rationale for using various lenses and editing techniques, as well as his method of working with Gerard Brach and his feelings about improvisation. His film school experience and films by others that shaped his own aesthetic views are touched upon, as are his views on the use of color and of the supernatural in film. Illustrated.

429 Anon. "*Chinatown*." *Films and Filming*, 20 (August), 25–27.
Photo essay with brief captions.

430 Anon. "*Chinatown*: Ice Cold." *Black Panther*, 12, no. 10 (28 September), 19.
Chinatown captures the "icy" treachery of capitalist businessmen in an "exciting, mysterious, fast-moving drama" according to this brief review.

*❋431** Anon. "*Chinatown*." *Independent Film Journal*, 74 (26 June), 7–8.
Cited in Aceto, Vincent, Jane Graves and Fred Silva, eds. *Film Literature Index*. Vol. 2. New York and London: R. R. Bowker, 1976, 95.

432 Anon. "*Chinatown*." *Mademoiselle*, 79, no. 5 (September), 139.
Brief review calls film "high gloss trash."

433 Anon. "*Chinatown*." *PTA Magazine*, 69 (November), 8.
Very brief review notes "confusing plot," "superior acting and directing," and effective mood.

*❋434** Anon. "*Chinatown*." *Takeover*, 4, no. 11 (18 September), 12.
Cited in *Alternate Press Index*. Vol. 6, no. 1. College Park, Maryland: Alternate Press Center, 1975, 38.

435 Anon. "Everybody's Doing the Whodunit." *New York Times* (8 December), II, p. 15.
Article credits success of *Chinatown* with spawning similar films.

436 Anon. "'Forget It Jake, It's *Chinatown*.'" *Films Illustrated*, 4 (September), 28–29.
Very brief picture caption concerning success of film. Illustrated.

437   Anon. "Jack Nicholson Massacre Faye Dunaway!" *Cine Revue* 54 (25 July), 4–5.
Photo essay on *Chinatown.*

438   Anon. "Polanski to Stage Berg Opera 'Lulu' at Spoleto Festival." *New York Times* (22 January), p. 35.
Brief news announcement of Polanski's debut as an opera director.

439   Anon. "The Current Scene: America: Polanski On *Chinatown.*" *Film* [Sheffield, England], Series 2, no. 19 (October), 20.
Brief summary of Polanski's interview at the AFI. *See* No. 428.

440   Anon. "Third time lucky." *The Times* [London] (11 April), p. 13.
Review of *What?* sees it as "tiresome, needlessly spun out, obvious and heavy-handed."

441   Ballad, Richard. "Penthouse Interview: Roman Polanski." *Penthouse,* 5 (August), 89–96.
Interview discusses Polanski's background, working methods, and relationships with actors, with specific references to *Knife in the Water, Chinatown,* and *The Fearless Vampire Killers.*

442   Baumbach, Jonathan. "Going to the Movies: Pieces of the Masters." *Partisan Review,* 41, no. 4, 581–83.
Chinatown is "an elegantly stylized homage" to the detective movie genre, which presents a "romantic vision of a murderously corrupt and impotent world." It deals with "the end of a mythic nobler time" and is filled with "moment to moment pleasures."

443   Beckwith, Nina. "Polanski's Debut As Stage Director At Spoleto A 'Lulu.'" *Variety* (26 June), pp. 2, 76.
News story contains quotes from Polanski dealing with stage versus screen directing.

*444   Belmans, J[acques]. "*Chinatown.*" *Amis du Film et de la Television,* no. 223 (December), p. 11.
Cited in Aceto, Vincent, Jane Graves and Fred Silva, eds. *Film Literature Index.* Vol. 2. New York and London: R. R. Bowker, 1976, 96.

445   Burke, Tom. "The Restoration of Roman Polanski." *Rolling Stone,* no. 165 (18 July), pp. 40–46.
Long interview feature focuses on *Chinatown* with quotes by Polanski about his problems and goals in making the film and an account of his working methods on the set. Reprinted in No. 566.

446   Burke, Tom. "What Directors Are Saying: Roman Polanski." *Action,* 9, no. 5 (September-October), 22.
Reprinted excerpts of No. 445.

447   Canby, Vincent. "A Summer Guide—Dillies and Duds." *New York Times* (28 July), II, pp. 1, 3.
Chinatown is recommended as "fun" if approached with "tempered expectations."

448 Canby, Vincent. "Polanski's *Chinatown* Views Crime of '30s." *New York Times* (21 June), p. 26.

Review sees *Chinatown* as "competently stylish, more or less thirtyish movie" that can't measure up to its predecessors *The Maltese Falcon* and *The Big Sleep*. Reprinted in No. 532.

°449 Canham, C. "*Chinatown*." *Audience*, 7 (November), 8–9.

Cited in Aceto, Vincent, Jane Graves and Fred Silva, eds. *Film Literature Index*. Vol. 2. New York and London: R. R. Bowker, 1976, 96.

450 Cargin, Peter. "*Chinatown*." *Film* [England], Series 2, no. 18 (September), p. 18.

In *Chinatown*, "Polanski seems to have been caught between the machinations of the intricate plot that his scriptwriter has given him and his controlled and well-composed visual style." The result is a film that "lacks a central core to sustain it, an attitude to the time, place and events to carry it through." Illustrated.

451 Cocks, Jay. "Lost Angelenos." *Time*, 104 (1 July), 42.

Review calls *Chinatown* an "exotic and cunning entertainment," but objects to film's lack of depth. Illustrated.

452 Cohen, M. S. "*Chinatown*." *Take One*, 4, no. 4 (July), 32.

In its direct homage to the private eye formula, yet "original variation on a form," *Chinatown* reveals more clearly than in many of his immediately previous works the complex talent of Polanski who "has pulled together a film that gains strength from its restraint and yet retains its ability to surprise."

453 Coleman, J. "Deep Waters." *New Statesman*, 88 (9 August), 197–98.

Review discusses twists and turns of *Chinatown*'s "practically unpursuable plot" in terms of individual clues. The film as a whole, in spite of Nicholon's performance, is "recalled as nerveless, as if seen from too great a distance, much less than the sum of its parts."

454 Coleman, J. "Wear the Gold Hat." *New Statesman*, 87 (19 April), 556.

Very brief review of *What?* criticizes the film as a hodge-podge of "sloppy nonsense."

455 Combs, Richard. "*Chinatown*." *Monthly Film Bulletin*, 41, no. 487 (August), 171–72.

Review considers film as "a solid, many-layered detective puzzle on lives intersecting in past, present and future."

456 Cook, P. "The sound track." *Films in Review*, 25, no. 9 (November), 560–63.

Article discusses events surrounding the writing of a musical score for *Chinatown* by Phillip Lambro and the factors relating to its removal from the film.

457 Crist, Judith. "One Summer of Happiness." *New York Magazine*, 7 (8 July), 74–75.

Chinatown is a "compliment to the taste and intelligence of the viewer" and shows Polanski "back to the clean-cut style of his earliest Polish films."

458 Cumbow, Robert C. *"Dance of the Vampires." Movietone News,* no. 33 (July), pp. 46–47.
Review calls film an "ambivalently comic, profoundly troubling sortie into cinema Gothic," praising it as "one of the most lyrical horror films ever made."

459 Dawson, Jan. *"Che? (What?)" Monthly Film Bulletin,* 41, no. 484 (May), 94–95.
Review sees film as "puerile graffito scrawled in the margins of its literary antecedents."

460 Elley, D. *"What?" Films and Filming,* 20 (June), 45.
Review considers film as "a modern version of *Alice in Wonderland,*" praising Polanski's "lazy style" of directing.

461 Elliott, D. *"Chinatown." Film Heritage,* 10, no. 1 (Fall), 44–46.
The film "sums up the oppression that many people feel about modern life." Polanski handles the story "seductively" and "captures the '30s [atmosphere] better than most '30s movies."

462 Farber, S[tephen]. "L. A. Journal." *Film Comment,* 10, no. 6 (November-December), 2.
Chinatown is considered as "a manufactured event," representing "a triumph of public relations over common sense."

463 Farber, Stephen. "Movies That Reflect Our Obsession With Conspiracy and Assassination." *New York Times* (11 August), II, pp. 11, 20.
Chinatown, considered as one of a group of films reflecting a national preoccupation with Watergate, is labeled "pretentious" and "paranoid"; analysis of *Chinatown* as an example of a film that presents heroism as "futile and irrelevant," thus reinforcing the "passivity of a jaded public." Reprinted in No. 535.

464 Forshay, G. "Exploring Uncharted Depths of Depravity." *Christian Century,* 91 (18 September), 860–61.
Chinatown is Polanski's bleakest film, "an acceptance of the total corruption of reality" that offers the individual no choice except to be part of the "grotesque perversity" that is post-Watergate America.

°465 Fuksiewicz, Jacek. *"Macbeth." Kultura,* no. 5, p. 10.
Cited by Filmoteka Polska; See No. 681. Illustrated.

466 Gans, Herbert J. *"Chinatown:* An Anticapitalist Murder Mystery." *Social Policy,* 5 (November-December), 48–49.
Chinatown offers a "somewhat more sensitive treatment of a real-world issue than is usual in Hollywood films, thanks to Robert Towne's screenplay." But the evils of capitalism are finally lost sight of by the movie's insistence on focusing blame on "one evil individual." The film's "theme of sexual pathology" also obscures the political message, because Cross, the Capitalist, is seen as more potent sexually than Mulwray or Gittes. Illustrated.

467 Gilliatt, Penelope. "Private Nose." *The New Yorker*, 50 (1 July), 70.
Review praises film as "wickedly skillful, funny, and socially alert."

468 Gow, Gordon. *"Chinatown." Films and Filming*, 21, no. 1 (October), 38–39.
Film "is primarily a rich affirmation of Roman Polanski's character as a director." "Implicitly darker" than earlier hard-boiled stories, it succeeds through a "leisurely accumulation of atmosphere . . . after an uncertain first 20 minutes." Of special interest are the qualities of the major performances and the film's "carefully planned colour scheme." Illustrated.

469 Gussow, Mel. "Only Faye Dunaway Knows What She's Hiding." *New York Times* (20 October), II, pp. 1, 17, 19.
Feature story on actress focuses on her methods of acting and problems on the set of *Chinatown*. Illustrated.

470 Hatch, Robert. *"Chinatown." The Nation*, 219 (6 July), 29–30.
Review praises *Chinatown* as "pop masterpiece" that overlays conventions of old detective films with "present fears and defeats."

471 Higham, Charles. "What Directors Are Saying: Roman Polanski." *Action*, 9, no. 1 (January-February), 38.
Reprinted excerpts of No. 410.

472 Hofler, Robert. "Films." *Penthouse*, 6 (September), 35–36.
Review of *Chinatown* sees it as blend of "the Thirties, the Forties and the Fifties," the purpose of which is "to document the decline of the American dream." Illustrated.

473 Houston, Penelope. "Polanski brings private eye bouncing back." *The Times* [London] (9 August), p. 9.
Review praises the way *Chinatown* handles the private eye formula by keeping "its sense of the past within itself." The film's water imagery and setting are also discussed. Illustrated.

*474 Jackiewicz, Aleksander. *"Macbeth." Życie Literackie*, no. 2, p. 15.
Cited by Filmoteka Polska; *See* No. 681. Illustrated.

475 Jameson, Richard T. "Film noir: Today; Son of Noir." *Film Comment*, 10, no. 6 (November-December), 30, 33.
Chinatown is a valid updating of the themes and motifs of *film noir*, notable for its "tremendous sense of *objets trouvés*" and for Faye Dunaway's portrayal of "the eminently untrustworthy, irresistibly alluring *film noir* female." Illustrated.

*476 Jameson, R[ichard] T. " 'Forget It, Jake, It's *Chinatown.*' " *Movietone News*, no. 33 (July), pp. 1–8.
Cited in Aceto, Vincent, Jane Graves and Fred Silva, eds. *Film Literature Index*. Vol. 2. New York and London: R. R. Bowker, 1976, 96.

*477 J. J. S. *"Macbeth." Tygodnik Powszechny*, no. 22, p. 6.
Cited by Filmoteka Polska; *See* No. 681.

478 Kael, Pauline. "On the Future of the Movies." *The New Yorker*, 50 (5 August), 43–59.
Brief remarks see *Chinatown's* presentation of life as "a blood-red maze" as one reason people are not attending movies as much as they formerly did. Reprinted in No. 579.

479 Kael, Pauline. "The Actor and the Star." *The New Yorker*, 50 (14 October), 175,
Brief comments on John Huston and Polanski as actors in *Chinatown*. Reprinted in No. 580.

480 Kaplan, F. "*Chinatown*." *Cineaste*, 6, no. 3, 38–39.
Review criticizes the film for its lack of complexity, which, though "technically impressive," only exploits the Watergate paranoia of its time solely for Polanski's profit—soothing the public into the "belief that impotence is *good* and, indeed, the only noble way out." Illustrated.

481 Kareda, Urjo. "Is There Any Future For Bad Taste." *New York Times* (18 August), II, pp. 1, 11.
Discussion of "desperate" attempts in current films to capture audiences' attention by exploiting the "shock effect" of "taboo" subjects cites the incest motif in *Chinatown* as a primary example. Reprinted in No. 543.

482 Kasindorf, Martin. "Hot Writer." *Newsweek*, 84 (14 October), 114–14B.
Screenwriter for *Chinatown* Robert Towne discusses his background, approach to his craft and difficult working relationship with Polanski. Illustrated.

483 Kauffmann, S[tanley]. "*Chinatown*." *The New Republic*, 171 (20 July), 16, 34.
Chinatown as Polanski's homage to pre-war Hollywood is "smartly directed," but needs to be "shorter and less consciously paradigmatic [to] be a good sinister thriller."

484 Kavanagh, James. "*Chinatown*: Other Places, Other Times." *Jump Cut*, no. 3 (September-October), pp. 1, 8.
In the film, Chinatown is seen as "a place outside the universe of bourgeois discourse." The period setting satisfies a nostalgic desire to recall a time "when the rich were really the rich." Though it insists "on the pervasiveness of the corruption of bourgeois life clear through to that sacred social core—the bourgeois family," it fails by presenting bourgeois society as "a natural rather than historical phenomenon." Illustrated.

485 Ledóchowski, Aleksander. "Życiorys z Nożem. *Film*, no. 3, p. 8.
In a discussion concerning *The Tenant*, Polanski explains his attitudes toward the main character and the film—not a farce, although the characters are "funny," and not a pathological study—"Trelkovsky is not insane; the surroundings are." Illustrated.

486 Martineau, Barbara Halpern. "*Chinatown's* Sexism." *Jump Cut*, no. 4 (November-December), p. 24.

Letter attacks essays on *Chinatown* by Kavanagh and Sperber for ignoring the role of women "whose oppression the film does pretend to capture but only to exploit it." Reprinted in No. 617.

487 Mason, A. "*Chinatown.*" *Peoples World*, 37, no. 28 (20 July), 10.
Very brief review outlines historical basis for *Chinatown* narrative in the California water swindle during the early part of the twentieth century, and refutes charges of its "escapism."

488 Milne, Tom. "*Chinatown.*" *Sight and Sound*, 43, no. 4 (Autumn), 243–44.
Reviewer feels that the discipline of Hollywood gives substance and form to Polanski's work, and in both *Rosemary's Baby* and *Chinatown* he "handles the mechanics of the plot with a ruthless brilliance that is immediately involving." Illustrated.

489 Murf. [Murphy, Arthur D.] "*Chinatown.*" *Variety* (19 June), p. 16.
Review praises film as "outstanding," giving special attention to Richard Sylbert's "magnificent" production design.

490 Oliver, N. "*Chinatown.*" *The Militant*, 38, no. 29 (26 July), 20.
Very brief review stresses the incorporation of Polanski's "uncanny ability to evoke a sense of terror and moral malaise" within the classic detective genre.

491 Pechter, William S. "Everyman in *Chinatown.*" *Commentary*, 58 (September), 71–73.
Review praises film's ability to "make a myth" of the Los Angeles of Chandlerian detective stories and sees the setting as "an adumbrative image of America itself," with the hero as an "American everyman."

492 Pielka, M. "*Chinatown.*" *Workers Power*, no. 4 (17 September), p. 13.
Chinatown represents a model for social order everywhere in which money determines treatment and relationships in a film which succeeds in "bringing real fear to the screen" because the audience empathizes with the characters whose fears are "grounded in reality."

493 Powell, Dilys. "The Eye of the Master." *Sunday Times* [London] (11 August), p. 23.
Brief review of *Chinatown* comments on its "tight, intentionally enigmatic script" and the "Chameleon" performance of Jack Nicholson. Illustrated.

494 Powell, Dilys. "The Great Enigma." *Sunday Times* [London] (14 April), p. 32.
Very brief review of *What?* calls it a "desperate farce."

495 Purdy, John. "*Chinatown.*" *Movietone News*, no. 34 (August), 37–38.
Review cites Polanski's ability to show "reverence" for Hollywood genres while revealing a "personal style" by "underplaying his drama with his camera or seasoning it with humor."

496 Reilly, Charles [Phillips]. "*Chinatown.*" *Films In Review*, 25, no. 7 (August-September), 442.

Very brief review of *Chinatown* as Polanski's best film since *Knife in the Water*, an "extraordinarily successful tour de force." Illustrated.

497 Rich, Frank. "A Lighter Shade of Hell." *New Times*, pp. 56–57, 62.
Article compares *Chinatown* to others of the detective game and concludes that "for all its elaborate machinations and extravagant production values, [the film] fails to contribute anything new in the way of perspective or understanding to a cultural mythos."

498 Rosenbaum, J[onathan]. "Paris-London Journal." *Film Comment*, 10, no. 6 (November-December), 4, 61.
Chinatown is considered as "the least personal film of Polanski's to date," as contrasted with *What?*, "a lark of a movie." Audiences and critics prefer *Chinatown* because of its "trendier" subject matter, "but craft and efficiency aren't the same thing as freshness or inspiration." Illustrated.

499 Rothwell, K[enneth] S. "A Reply to Mr. Silverstein." *Literature/ Film Quarterly*, 2, no. 1, 91–92.
Reply to criticism of interpretation of opening shot of *Macbeth*.

500 Ruszkowski, A. "*Chinatown*." *Séquences*, 19, no. 78 (October), 34–35.
Brief review of *Chinatown* compares it in technique and "world view" to Polanski's first feature *Knife in the Water*.

501 Sarris, Andrew. "*Chinatown* and Polanski-Town: Tilting Toward Tragedy." *The Village Voice*, 19 (7 November), 85.
Chinatown shows that Polanski is at his best "destroying the illusions of others" in collaborative efforts rather than "rendering his own pessimism" in personal projects.

502 Sarris, Andrew. "Feeding at the Trivia Trough (*Chinatown*)." *The Village Voice*, 19 (1 August), 63.
A very brief note by Sarris admonishes readers to see *Chinatown* immediately—he will thoroughly analyze it later as it is "too complex for a consumer consultant review."

503 Sayre, Nora. "New Films Focus on California and Californians." *New York Times* (1 September), II, pp. 9, 19.
Essay on *Chinatown* and *California Split*, cites Polanski's evocation of California "through its landscape rather than its inhabitants. Illustrated. Reprinted in No. 555.

504 Segond, J. "Les anges du péché (*Chinatown*)." *Positif*, no. 164 (December), pp. 51–54.
Review presents synopsis of major themes of *Chinatown* (religious-mythical implications, water symbolism, etc.) contained in a successful resurrection of the private eye genre.

505 Silber, I. "*Chinatown*." *Guardian*, 26, no. 39 (10 July), 18.
Very brief review stresses waste of talent in film to "little contemporary avail."

506 Silverstein, N. "The Opening Shot of Roman Polanski's '*Macbeth.*'" *Literature/Film Quarterly*, 2, no. 1 (Winter), 88–90.
Brief article argues against the misreading of the "long take" opening *Macbeth* and its "fluid" eloquence.

507 Simon, John. "*Chinatown.*" *Esquire*, 82 (October), 14, 16.
Review praises *Chinatown* as "skillfully updated version" of detective genre, but states that its fidelity to generic conventions prevents it from having "full character development."

508 Sperber, Murray. " 'Do as little as possible.' Polanski's Message and Manipulation." *Jump Cut*, no. 3 (September-October), pp. 9–10.
Chinatown shows Polanski as a "barqoue" artist, and its "vision of corruption and nihilism" gives "Polanski's recipe for declining America: lean back and don't fight it, enjoy its decadent art." Gittes, as the "petty-bourgeois," exposes the corruption of capitalism (the sexual as well as the financial). Illustrated.

509 Sragow, Michael. "*Chinatown*: The Roman Version." *New York Magazine*, 7 (26 August), 54.
Review praises film's "solid script," but objects to its "embalming craftsmanship." The historical incident that formed the basis of the movie's political plot is described, but Towne's concern for the land is lost in Polanski's direction, which "never lets in any air."

510 Terlecki, Marian. "*Macbeth.*" *Tygodnik Morski*, no. 6, p. 18.
Macbeth continues Polanski's exploration of the same conflict begun in *Knife in the Water*: that of a young man challenging the "old" world.

511 Turan, Kenneth. "In Chandler Country." *The Progressive*, 38 (September), 53–54.
Review praises *Chinatown*'s fidelity to the spirit of Chandler in the "pull" of its plot and the "evocative" portrayal of 1930's Los Angeles.

512 Walling, William. "*Chinatown.*" *Society*, 12 (November), 73–77.
As a variation on the hard-boiled detective formula, *Chinatown* uses its 1930's setting to suggest "the unified city where hardboiled detective fiction has always been most at home," while offering "an implicit explanation for the decline of the genre itself—the continued reckless expansion of our cities through motives no more enlightened than the calculations of economic self-interest." Illustrated.

513 Weiler, A. H. "Film Critics Cite *Amarcord* and Fellini." *New York Times* (31 December), p. 12.
Brief news story includes account of choice of Jack Nicholson as best actor of the year for *Chinatown* and *The Last Detail* by the New York Film Critics Circle.

514 Westerbeck, C[olin] L., Jr. "The Small Sleep." *Commonweal*, 100 (26 July), 405.
Review of *Chinatown* discusses the film's debt to *The Big Sleep* and criticizes its attempt to appear both original and a "trendy" commercial hit—"the entire film is a bunch of contradictory impressions alternated with outbursts of sex and violence."

515 Whitman, Mark. *"Chinatown." Films Illustrated,* 3 (August), 472.
Brief review sees film as failed nostalgia, saved only by "the trio of
central performances." Illustrated.

516 Wilmington, M. "Roman Polanski's *Chinatown." Velvet Light Trap,*
no. 13 (Fall), 13–16.
Chinatown represents Polanski's venture into the world of Chandler and
Hammett, "the battleground of the cynical outsider and the guilty rich";
a recreation of the "perfect model" of the private eye film. Elments of
political intrigue and romance are interwoven in the plot, "making a
cause-and-effect of private anguish and public scandal," presenting neither
"simple nostalgic affirmation or simple pity," but a lament for doomed
characters which Polanski presents with "fastidious precision" and "im-
maculate drollery." Illustrated.

517 Zimmerman, Paul D. "Blood and Water." *Newsweek,* 84 (1 July), 74.
Review praises film as "story about decadence of '70s," though "inner
lives" of characters are touched on too lightly. Includes quotes by the
director concerning his fascination with genres. Illustrated.

1974-1975

518 Stewart, Garrett. *"The Long Goodbye* from *Chinatown." Film
Quarterly,* 28, no. 2 (Winter), 25–32.
The "satiric thrust" of Polanski's film "is clear only if we see it pointing
forward in time . . . to the metropolitan blight of *The Long Goodbye."*
Both films take their "emotional center from the mentality of their
heroes," who are, in each case, "a fundamental revision of the detective
stereotype." Polanski and Towne have also learned much from Altman's
"freedom with dialogue and detail," so that in *Chinatown* "a sense of
atmospheric foreboding divorced from plot, and more importantly, . . . a
suspension in symbolic details . . . defines the true plot line of the film."
Illustrated.

1975

519 Alonzo, J. A. "Behind the scenes of *Chinatown." American Cinema-
tographer,* 26, no. 5 (May), 526–29, 564–65, 572–73, 585–91.
Director of Photography who replaced Stanley Cortez after two weeks
of shooting discusses his rapport with and respect for Polanski and his
technical abilities, and the modern technology which they applied to
the filming of a "classic mystery film" while "studiously avoiding gimmicks
and self-conscious techniques." Illustrated.

520 Anon. *"Chinatown* and *Express* Top 1974 Awards Nominations for
'Stellas.'" *Variety* (5 February), p. 28.
Article lists nominations for awards from the Society of Film and
Television Arts.

521 Anon. *"Chinatown* Wins Most Golden Globe Awards." *Boxoffice,*
106 (3 February), 10.
Brief news item.

522 Anon. "La Presse." *Avant-Scene*, no. 154 (January), pp. 50–51.
Excerpts from reviews of *The Fearless Vampire Killers* by Phillippe Haudiquet, Henry Chapier, Jean de Baroncelli, Jean Nareoni, Jean-Loup Passek, and Claude Michel Cluny.

523 Anon. *"Le Bal des Vampires."* *Avant-Scene*, no. 154 (January), pp. 2–4.
Credits, a reproduction of an advertising poster, and production notes on the film. Illustrated.

524 Anon. *"Le Bal des Vampires*: Texte Integral." *Avant-Scene*, no. 154 (January), pp. 6–50.
The complete text of the 107-minute version of the film translated into French, including dialogue and stage directions. Followed by notes on the text. Illustrated.

525 Anon. "Nicholson, Polanski Promo Tours Help Lift *Chinatown* Biz." *Variety* (5 February), p. 28.
Brief news story tells of director's trips to South America, Australia, and the Far East to promote film.

526 Anon. "Par *Chinatown* Sock Big O'Seas Handled by CIC; Figures Given." *Variety* (29 January), p. 41.
Brief news story.

527 Anon. "Pravda Says Money Determines Oscars." *New York Times* (9 June), p. 46.
Brief news story mentions *Chinatown* as movie that glorifies crime.

528 Anon. "Two Films Dominate Oscar Nominations." *New York Times* (25 February), p. 31.
Brief news story cites major award nominations for *Chinatown*. Illustrated.

529 Baryshnikov, Mikhail et al. "Some Favorites Pick Their Favorites." *New York Times* (5 January), II, p. 13.
Chinatown listed among best movies of year by various celebrities.

530 Benoit, C. *"Chinatown."* *Jeune Cinéma*, 84 (February), 38–40.
Chinatown is a "respectful homage" to American *film noir*, a new and original work in its portrayal of the two parallel investigations which reveal economic, political and moral corruption.

531 Canby, Vincent. "Critic's Choice: The Eleven Best Films of 1974." *New York Times* (5 January), II, p. 13.
Chinatown listed as runner-up.

532 Canby, Vincent. "Polanski's *Chinatown* Views Crime of '30s." *New York Times Film Reviews 1973–1974*. New York: The New York Times and Arno Press, p. 224.
Reprint of No. 448.

533   Canby, Vincent. *"What?" New York Times Film Reviews 1973–1974.*
New York: The New York Times and Arno Press, p. 112.
Reprint of No. 402.

534   Cluny, Claude Michel. *"Chinatown." Cinéma* 75 [Paris], no. 194
(January), pp. 142–43.
Review calls *Chinatown* "extremely beautiful," but not up to the level
of Polanski's early films. The final scene evokes a "funereal madness,"
but the movie fails to work together as a whole. Illustrated.

535   Farber, Stephen. " 'Conspiracy' Movies." *New York Times Film
Reviews 1973–1974.* New York: The New York Times and Arno Press,
pp. 248–49.
Reprint of No. 463.

536   Grangé, Michèle. *"Chinatown." Téléciné*, no. 197 (March), pp. 29–30.
Brief review calls film "thin" and suggests that Polanski is "overrated."

537   Hepnerová, E. *"Chinatown." Film A Doba*, 21, no. 5 (May),
pp. 280–81.
Using *The Long Goodbye* as a particular comparison point, reviewer
concludes that *Chinatown* lacks multi-dimensionality, particularly of the
script, which follows Chandler's literary style too closely and doesn't
offer a dramatically different interpretation in terms of the film and
becomes too long and "talky." Illustrated.

538   Jorgens, J. "The opening scene of Polanski's *Macbeth.*" *Literature/
Film Quarterly*, 3, no. 3 (Summer), 277–78.
Comments continue exchange concerning opening shot of *Macbeth*.

539   Kael, Pauline. "Beverly Hills as a Big Bed." *The New Yorker*, 51
(17 February), 90, 93.
Brief comments on Robert Towne's contributions to *Chinatown*. Reprinted in No. 578.

540   Kané, Pascal. "La ville des feintes (*Chinatown*)." *Cahiers Du
Cinéma*, no. 256 (February-March), pp. 63–64.
As an indictment of corrupt capitalist America, *Chinatown* both disgusts
with its depiction of the moral impoverishment of the film's metaphoric
title and fascinates with its treatment of primitive violence and death
in a form which skillfully exploits "le thriller" genre.

541   Kané, Pascal. "Une Demystification du Vampirisme." *Avant-Scene*,
no. 154 (January), p. 5.
As one of Polanski's most successful films, *The Fearless Vampire Killers*
exemplifies much about its director's concerns, because of his sympathy
with the vampire genre. But his treatment of vampires is less mystical
than is traditional, both in terms of his portrayal of them as a social
group and his depiction of their sexuality.

542   Kaplan, H. S. *"Chinatown." Landscape Architecture*, 65 (April), 222.
Review of *Chinatown* as "notable not only for its unusual premise in land
planning, but also for its exceptional execution as a film."

543 Kareda, Urjo. "Is There Any Future For Bad Taste." *New York Times Film Reviews 1973–1974*. New York: The New York Times and Arno Press, pp. 250–51.
Reprint of No. 481.

544 Kauffmann, Stanley. *"Macbeth,"* in his *Living Images: Film Comment and Criticism*. New York: Harper, pp. 90–92.
Reprint of No. 383.

545 Lefèvre, R[aymond]. *"Chinatown." Image et Son*, no. 293 (February), pp. 88–90.
Review considers film as an homage to the *film noir* of the forties which goes further than its models by providing for a tragic conclusion. The symbolic role of the title and of water are also considered. Illustrated.

546 McGinnis, W. D. *"Chinatown*: Roman Polanski's contemporary Oedipus Story." *Literature/Film Quarterly*, 3, no. 3 (Summer), 249–51.
Comparison of *Chinatown* and *Oedipus Rex* stresses the "wasteland motif" and "atmosphere of decay" that predominates both. *Chinatown* is outstanding in its illumination of the "deepest responses of the imagination." Illustrated.

547 Michalek, Boleslaw. "Naddatek." *Kino*, no. 6 (June), pp. 58–59.
The story and audience of *Chinatown* benefit from the inclusion of elements from a strange and exotic culture within good Hollywood moviemaking. Illustrated.

*548 M. M. "Gwalt Nie Jest Dla Mnie Sensacja." *Życie Literackie*, no. 4, p. 15.
Cited by Filmoteka Polska; *See* No. 681. Illustrated.

*549 Offroy, D. *"Chinatown." Cinematographe*, no. 11 (January-February), p. 2.
Cited in Aceto, Vincent, Jane Graves and Fred Silva, eds. *Film Literature Index*. Vol. 3. New York and London: R. R. Bowker, 1977, 101.

550 Oliver, B. *"The Long Goodbye* and *Chinatown*: Debunking the Private Eye Tradition." *Literature/Film Quarterly*, 3, no. 3 (Summer), 240–48.
The unexpected re-emergence of the private eye in films emphasizes the satire of the subject and "does not coincide with a reaffirmation of the value of positive action." Comparison of detective fiction and recent film treatments concludes that "Altman and Polanski are more faithful to the complexity of the malaise," but in this "realism" the hero is not equipped to deal with such all-pervasive evil: in Polanski's film he is only a "gifted amateur" doomed to failure by the director's loss of faith in his "knightly" code. Illustrated.

551 Perret, Jacques G. "Biofilmographie Roman Polanski." *Avant-Scene*, no. 154 (January), pp. 52–57.
Contains a brief biography, complete acting and directing credits and plot summaries of the films. Illustrated.

552 Polanski, Roman. *Three Films.* London: Lorrimer Publishing.
Scripts of *Knife in the Water, Cul-De-Sac,* and *Repulsion* with introduction by Boleslaw Sulik. Critical Appendix includes reprints of excerpts of Nos. 82, 198, 218, 295.

*553 Randall, M. "*Chinatown.*" *Cinema Papers,* 2 (March-April), 51–52.
Cited in Aceto, Vincent, Jane Graves and Fred Silva, eds. *Film Literature Index.* Vol. 3. New York and London: R. R. Bowker, 1977, 101.

554 Rogowski, Zbigniew. "Lódzkiej Szkole Zawdzieczam Wszystko."
Przekrój, no. 1587, pp. 8–11.
Polanski discusses the importance and influences of the Lodz Film School and a personal assessment of his films. Illustrated.

555 Sayre, Nora. "New Films Focus on California and Californians."
New York Times Film Reviews 1973–1974. New York: The New York Times and Arno Press, pp. 259–60.
Reprint of No. 503.

556 T[essier], M. "La Griffe du Passé." *Ecran,* no. 32 (January),
pp. 63–64.
Chinatown represents not only a conscious reworking of an old genre, but "an elegant and sophisticated variation" although without "soul."

*557 Thingvall, J. "*Chinatown.*" *Cinefantastique,* 4, no. 1, 32.
Cited in Aceto, Vincent, Jane Graves and Fred Silva, eds. *Film Literature Index.* Vol. 3. New York and London: R. R. Bowker, 1977, 101.

558 Wajda, Andrzej. "Polanski: Faire des Films en Pologne ou Ailleurs."
Jeune Cinéma, 91 (December), 10–13.
Translation of No. 391.

1975-1976

559 Canby, Vincent. "When Coyness Becomes a Cop-Out." *New York Times Film Reviews 1975–1976.* New York: The New York Times and Arno Press, pp. 226–27.
Reprint of No. 567.

1976

560 Alvarez, A. "Will Polanski Make a Star of Polanski?" *New York Times* (22 February), II, pp. 1, 15.
Feature interview with Polanski focuses on filming of *The Tenant* and his feelings about playing the dual role of actor and director.

561 Anon. "*Lokator w Pułapce.*" *Film* [Warsaw], 4 (15 February), 12–13.
Polanski discusses his double duties as director and actor in the title role of *The Tenant,* his first film made in Paris.

*562 Anon. "Ponure Dzielnice." *Życie Warszawy,* no. 190 (11 August).
Cited by Filmoteka Polska; *See* No. 681.

563 Anon. "White house protest on TV film." *The Times* [London] (28 August), p. 20.

News story tells of protest over the BBC's decision to show *Rosemary's Baby*.

564 Bartholomew, David. "*The Tenant.*" *Film Information* (July-August), p. 4.

Brief review calls film "a case study, frozen with literary overtones," and objects to the "sourness" of Polanski's world view.

565 Bartholomew, David. "Polanski: *The Tenant.*" *Cinefantastique*, 5, no. 3, 4–7, 30.

Review focuses on the way Trelkovsky's apartment and building become "a major active character" in the film and on how the director constructs the last half of the action so that the viewer finds it difficult "to distinguish fantasy from fact."

A question-and-answer interview with Polanski follows, in which the director discusses specific details of lighting, set design, and camera angles, as well as recounting the history of the film's production. Illustrated.

566 Burke, Tom. *Burke's Steerage*. New York: G. P. Putnam, pp. 35–36. Reprint of No. 445.

567 Canby, Vincent. "When Coyness Becomes a Cop-Out." *New York Times* (27 June), II, p. 15.

Unlike films in the current fad of the "put-on," lacking any commitment to material, *The Tenant* represents the style, wit, and originality of an artist who "intellectualizes experiences" and accepts responsibility for his work. Reprinted in No. 559.

568 Castle, William. *Step Right Up! I'm Gonna Scare the Pants Off America*. New York: Putnam, pp. 185–217.

The producer of *Rosemary's Baby* recalls the experience of working with Polanski.

569 Cocks, Jay. "Furn. Apt. to Let." *Time*, 108 (26 July), 68.

As "a comedy tipped with poison," *The Tenant* reveals Polanski's distinctly Absurdist vision. Illustrated.

570 Combs, Richard. "Conspiracy of horrors." *The Times* [London] (3 September), p. 7.

Review praises *The Tenant*'s Kafka-esque quality but objects to its superficial rendering of the psychosexual element during the second half.

571 Crist, Judith. "Shtick by Simon, Paranoia by Polanski." *Saturday Review*, 3 (24 July), 42–43.

Review claims *The Tenant* is "awkwardly dubbed" and "a near-parody of Polanski's *Repulsion*."

572 Crouch, William. "Satanism and Possession in Selected Contemporary Novels and Their Cinematic Adaptations." Ph.D. dissertation, Northwestern University, pp. 37–64

Chapter on *Rosemary's Baby*, novel and film, concludes that the Polanski version is "most probably an exception to the rule in film adaptation—a film following the original novel in mood, character, point of view, motivation and plot sequence almost identically."

573 Cybulski, Wladyslaw. "Dwié Godziny z Romanem Polańskim." *Dziennik Polski*, no. 297 (30 December).
Polanski says that his filmic interests lie in showing action taking place within a small group of characters, ensnared in unusual situations.

574 Delmas, J[ean]. *"Le Locataire."* *Jeune Cinéma*, 96 (July-August), 26–27.
Although a less ambitious work than *Chinatown*, *The Tenant* is a film of high quality which recreates brilliantly its French ambience, and its great success lies in the "almost impalpable" means by which the audience is carried within Trelkovsky's anguish so that reality and fantasy are indistinguishable.

575 Gilliatt, Penelope. "Only a Lodger." *The New Yorker*, 52 (5 July), 62.
Review of *The Tenant* considers it as "the story of a man's short rental on his own span"; a film concerning exile from everything including self.

576 Gow, Gordon. *"The Tenant."* *Films and Filming*, 23, no. 1 (October), 31–32.
Review praises film's "realistic" but "discreet" study of paranoia. Illustrated.

577 Hatch, Robert. *"Films."* *The Nation*, 223 (17 July), 60.
Review of *The Tenant* objects that audience "cannot relate to subjective films about madness."

578 Kael, Pauline. "Beverly Hills as a Big Bed," in her *Reeling*. New York: Warner, pp. 584–85.
Reprint of No. 539.

579 Kael, Pauline. "On the Future of the Movies," in her *Reeling*. New York: Warner, p. 418.
Reprint of No. 478.

580 Kael, Pauline. "The Actor and the Star," in her *Reeling*. New York: Warner, p. 469.
Reprint of No. 479.

581 Kalużyński, Zygmunt. "Zbrodnia Jak Poezja." *Polityka*, no. 36 (9 April).
Excellent in its portrayal of unique characters, *Chinatown*'s success lies in the viewer's discovery of the basic immorality of life in which there is no meaning to justice, won or lost.

582 Kauffmann, S[tanley]. "Pleasantries, Mostly." *The New Republic*, 175 (7 August), 27.
Very brief review of *The Tenant* as a "beaut of a mistake" in which the "laborious attempts to frighten us . . . fail because we never care for the hero."

*583 Kolodziejczyk, Leszek. "Opetany Filmem." *Polityka*, no. 51, p. 9.
Cited by Filmoteka Polska; *See* No. 681. Illustrated.

584 Kuczewski, Maciej. "Film Jest Historiq Mego Życia." *Gazeta Południowa*, no. 296 (12 December).
In this interview Polanski states that "film is a history of [his] life" in which his interests lie in showing inter-relationships, usually in specific situations, taking place in limited space, or in not everyday conditions."

*585 Kuczewski, Maciej. "Jeszcze Nie Nakrecilem 'Mojęgo Filmu?'" *Życie Wardzawy*, no. 309, p. 7.
Cited by Filmoteka Polska; *See* No. 681.

586 Ledóchowski, Aleksander. "*Lokator.*" *Film* [Warsaw], no. 30 (25 July), p. 22.
Through *The Tenant* and the personality of Trelkovsky, Polanski reflects the battle in life between the "real and actual" and the "unreal and unreachable."

*587 Ledóchowski, Aleksander. "Lokatorzy *Lokatora.*" *Film*, no. 35, pp. 20–22.
Cited by Filmoteka Polska; *See* No. 681. Illustrated.

588 Lipiński, Andrzej. "Polański Retro." *Ekran*, 38 (19 September), 9.
Unlike pre-World War II American films in which the individual had the right to be, *Chinatown* represents the commercial movie which gives the audience "ready receipts for protecting order" and silently observing the prevailing rules: the "Great American Order" will survive attacks by lone, ambitious individuals.

589 M[aslin], J[anet]. "Jump!" *Newsweek*, 87 (28 June), 78.
Brief review condemns *The Tenant* as unintentional "self parody" on Polanski's part.

590 Maslin, Janet, et al. "*Tenant, The.*" *Film Review Digest*, 2, no. 1 (Fall), 89–90.
Excerpts from reviews in *Newsweek, New York Post, Los Angeles Times,* and *New York Magazine.*

591 Metrak, Krzysztof. "Bezprawi w Mieście Aniolów." *Kultura*, 32 (8 August).
Chinatown is Polanski's most impersonal film—a reflective copy of earlier private detective films distinguished from them by its attack on the political establishment which tolerates corruption in a society in which money frees people from responsibility.

592 Milne, Tom. "*Locataire, Le (The Tenant).*" *Monthly Film Bulletin*, 43, no. 512 (September), 193.
Review cites film's "Kafka"-like quality, objecting that it gradually falls off after a "brilliant" opening that expresses "subjective impressions through objective means." Though the opening "merges several levels of perception," Polanski later opts for "subjective camera and Grand Guignol." Illustrated (cover).

593 Niecikowski, Jerzy. "Gabinet Figur Woskowych." *Film*, 34 (22 August), 5.

Although noted for its talented direction and acting, *Chinatown* lacks tempo and presents an anachronistic vision of the world—a beautiful film lacking life, peopled with "wax figures."

594 Oakes, Philip. "Hallucinations, With Love." *Sunday Times* [London] (15 February), p. 35

Brief feature article researched on the set of *The Tenant* includes quotes from Polanski on a number of topics, including the violence in his films. Illustrated.

595 Overbey, David. "Polanski as Actor." *Sight and Sound*, 45, no. 2 (Spring), 84.

Article recounts background details on writing and filming *The Tenant* including Polanski discussing directing himself and aspects of working with a multi-lingual cast.

596 Paxton, Anne. "*Chinatown*." *Movietone News*, no. 34 (August), pp. 37–38.

Review praises film as "good mystery," leading to the conclusion that "non-involvement" has a "peculiar, deadly correctness."

597 Powell, Dilys. "Festival Feast." *Sunday Times* [London] (30 May), p. 37.

Very brief review calls *The Tenant* a comedy turned "ugly."

598 Powell, Dilys. "The Edge of Horror." *Sunday Times* [London] (29 August), p. 26.

Review of *The Tenant* calls it "the best of [Polanski's] horror movies," but objects to the "self-indulgent, over-explicit, suffocating" final scene.

599 Ratajczak, Mirosław. "*Chinatown*." *Wiadomości*, no. 45 (4 November).

Chinatown presents universal human truths in an excellently told story of the acquisition of power; a process of moral decay, brought about in a system that prefers the power of money.

600 Reilly, Charles Phillips. "*The Tenant*." *Films in Review*, 27, no. 7 (August-September), 441–42.

Review calls film "self-indulgent" and claims that the screenplay has a faulty rationale.

601 Robitaille, L. B. "Polanski tourne 'Le Locataire.'" *Ecran*, 45 (March), 4–5.

During filming of *The Tenant*, Polanski reveals the elements of his life and personality which his films reflect: "introversion, anxiety and irony."

602 Rosenbaum, Jonathan. "*The Tenant*." *Sight and Sound*, 45, no. 4 (Autumn), 253.

Review claims that spirit of "apathy" and "stylistic pirouette" characterized *The Tenant*. The film is made up of two dissociated sections, the "formalist," which dominates the first half, and the "black humor" of madness in the second. Illustrated.

603 Sarris, Andrew. "Horrors! The World Is Coming to an End." *The Village Voice*, 21, no. 28 (12 July), 115.

Review objects to *The Tenant*'s "lack of a consistent point of view," claiming it degenerates into "feeble outlandishness." Polanski is "ill-cast" as the hero. Illustrated.

604 Sherman, Eric. *Directing The Film*. Boston: Little, Brown and Company, pp. 44, 79, 110, 118, 181, 206, 214, 217–21, 250–51, 327–28.

Material from seminars at American Film Institute includes comments by Polanski on such topics as scriptwriting, acting, use of lenses, editing and film education. Reprint of excerpts from No. 428.

605 Simon, John. "Untenable *Tenant*." *New York Magazine* (28 June), pp. 66–68.

Long review considers *The Tenant* in relation to Polanski's past work, arguing that a "controlling factor" is necessary for him to produce superior films. Lacking such control in *The Tenant*, he created a work suffering from an "improbable story," explicit and naive technique, and clumsy dubbing.

606 Solomon, Stanley J. *Beyond Formula: American Film Genres*. New York, Chicago, San Francisco, and Atlanta: Harcourt, pp. 149-52, 236-40.

Rosemary's Baby is discussed in terms of its Hitchcockian blend of comedy and horror, and *Chinatown* is considered as a relatively conventional reworking of the hard-boiled detective genre, except for its "unexpected" ending. Illustrated.

607 Tuckman, Mitch. "Exiled on Main Street." *The Village Voice*, 21, no. 30 (26 July), 108.

Biographical sketch of Polanski as a "little tramp . . . born of intolerance, exile, and international vagrancy." Includes a brief review of *The Tenant* and its Kafkaesque "obsessive fear of being transformed." Illustrated.

608 Westerbeck, Colin L., Jr. "Rosemary's Booby." *Commonweal*, 103 (27 August), 563–64.

Review calls *The Tenant* "ultimately undecipherable," vacillating uncertainly between comedy and horror.

609 Wexman, Virginia Wright. "The Hard-Boiled Detective on Film." Ph.D. dissertation, University of Chicago, pp. 142–87.

Chapter on *Chinatown* shows how film shapes the conventions of the hard-boiled detective story into a tragic pattern.

610 Winiarczyk, Mirosław. "*Chinatown*: Incydent w Chińskiej Dzielnicy." *Ekran*, no. 34 (22 August), p. 21.

A harmonious film both dramatically and visually, *Chinatown* pinpoints the difficulty of psychological relationships between people.

611 Wiśniewski, Cezary. "Magia Chinskiej Dzielnicy." *Film* [Warsaw], no. 33 (15 August), p. 7.

Polanski rivals Hitchcock in his abilities as a director of suspense films. However, *Chinatown* fails as a critique of society in the Roosevelt era.

1977

612 Anon. "Polanski In Guilty Plea To Sex Felony; Deportation Cloud." *Variety* (10 August), pp. 2, 69.
News story includes information on director's future film projects.

613 Glowacki, Janusz. "Polo Potrafi." *Kultura*, no. 3 (16 January), pp. 1, 14.
Interview covers Polanski's feelings for French urbanites, as reflected in *The Tenant*, and topics of loneliness and alienation. Illustrated.

614 Górzanski, Jerzy. "Biedny Trelkovsky." *Film* [Warsaw], no. 48 (27 November), p. 10.
The Tenant depicts the "shocking" elements of life—loneliness, danger, terror, intolerance—which reflect Polanski's early traumas and personal concerns.

615 Kijowski, Janusz. "Sublokator." *Kultura*, no. 46 (13 November).
The Tenant reflects a clinical, though artificial and naive, study of sickness—Trelkovsky's grotesque death is the death of an artificial hero, who chose for himself an artificial life as an eternal subtenant.

616 Leach, James. "Notes on Polanski's Cinema of Cruelty." *Wide Angle*, 1, no. 4, 56–57.
Brief notes dispute interpretation of Polanski's films as "a self-portrait," focuses instead on them as an "assemblage of signs and images designed to break down the conscious and cultural defenses of the audience." Reprinted in No. 629.

617 Martineau, Barbara Halpern. "Documenting the Patriarchy, *China-town*," in *Women and the Cinema*. Edited by Karyn Kay and Gerald Peary. New York: E. P. Dutton, pp. 347–51.
Reprint of No. 486.

618 Milne, Tom, et al. *"Tenant, The (Le Locataire)." Film Review Digest*, 2, no. 2 (Winter), 210–13.
Excerpts from reviews in *Monthly Film Bulletin, Saturday Review, Commonweal, Village Voice, Christian Science Monitor, Sunday Times* [London], *The Nation, Films in Review, Film Information, Women's Wear Daily* and *The Times* [London]

619 Niecikowski, Jerzy. "Zabawny Lokator." *Film* [Warsaw], no. 44 (30 October), p. 5.
Beneath the stability of life normality is always in danger from sickness, brutal strength, and insanity—and the insanity beneath everyday events causes Trelkovsky's madness.

*‎**620** Nowak, Leopold. "Spotkanie z Romanem Polańskim." *Przekrój*, no. 1658, p. 9.
Cited by Filmoteka Polska; See No. 681. Illustrated.

621 Palmer, R. Barton. *"Chinatown* and the Detective Story." *Literature/Film Quarterly*, 5, no. 2 (Spring), 112–17.

Film is compared to *Oedipus the King* to show how it has "transformed the detective story" by bringing out the "incipient self-doubts" of a period very much like the Sophoclean age. Illustrated.

622 Prendergast, Roy M. "From 1950 to the Present," in his *A Neglected Art*. New York: New York University Press, pp. 158–62.
Interview with composer Jerry Goldsmith focuses on how the music for *Chinatown* was created and contradicts information given in Sarris's review of the film. Illustrated.

623 Robak, Tadeusz. "Wszyscy Jesteśmy Lokatorami." *Życie Literackie*, no. 46 (13 November).
As a movie "magician," Polanski fascinates the audience with the film's suspense and narrative tone as well as interest in strange, unknown surroundings in which "we are all tenants."

624 Rosenbaum, Jonathan. "*Tenant, The (Le Locataire)*." *Film Review Digest*, 2, no. 3 (Spring), 336.
Excerpt from review in *Sight and Sound*.

625 Rumel, Witold. "*Lokator*: Brawurowe Kłamstwo Romana Polanskiego." *Ekran*, no. 49 (4 December), p. 21.
Rumel argues that Polanski's portrayal of Trelkovsky's life and neighbors in *The Tenant* represents a "lie" told with great style, but without accuracy, from outside the situation—a tale of "a group of insane tenants living in a nonexistent house."

*626 Skolimowski, Jerzy. "Wywiady Mnie Nuġa." *Kulisy*, no. 3 (16 January).
Cited by Filmoteka Polska; *See* No. 681.

627 Slowikowski, Bogdan. "Nigdy Nie Rezyserowalem Dla TV." *Życie Warszawy*, no. 9, p. 6.
In this brief interview Polanski discusses his disinterest in television, and working on *Chinatown*. Illustrated.

1978

628 Anon. "Polanski Flees Sex Sentencing." *Variety* (8 February,) p. 24.
Announcement of director's flight from the country to avoid sentencing for sex offense. Dino De Laurentiis's plan to replace Polanski with Jan Troell on *Hurricane* is also mentioned.

629 Leach, James. "Notes on Polanski's Cinema of Cruelty." *Wide Angle*, 2, no. 1, 32–39.
Notes of previous issue are reprinted as introduction to expanded discussion of the elements of Polanski's films which assault the security of the audience with the "underlying unity" of cruelty and violence beneath everyday life. Includes reprint of No. 616.

List of Performances and Writings

FILM PERFORMANCES

630 1953 *Three Stories (Trzy Opowiesci)* as Maly
    d: Konrad Nalecki, Ewa Poleska, Czeslaw Petelski

631 1954 *A Generation (Pokolenie)* as Mundek
    d: Andrzej Wajda

632 1955 *The Enchanted Bicycle (Zaczarowany Rower)* as Adas
    d: Silik Sternfeld

633 1956 *End of the Night (Koniec Wojny)* as Maly
    d: Julian Dziedzina, Pawel Komorowski, Walentyna Uszycka

634 1957 *Wrecks (Wraki)*
    d: Ewa and Czeslaw Petelski

635 1958 *Phone My Wife (Zadzwoncie Do Mojej Zony)*
    d: Jaroslav Mach

636 1958 *Two Men and a Wardrobe (Dwaj Ludzie Z Szasa)*
    d: Roman Polanski

637 1959 *Lotna* as Bandsman
    d: Andrzej Wajda

638 1959 *When Angels Fall (Gdy Spadaja Anioly)* as Old Woman
    d: Roman Polanski

639 1960 *Innocent Sorcerers (Niewinni Czarodzieje)* as Dudzio
    d: Andrzej Wajda

640 1960 *See You Tomorrow (Do Widzenia Do Jutra)* as Romek
    d: Janusz Morgenstern

641 1960 *Bad Luck (Zezowate Szczescie)*
    d: Andrzej Munk

642 1960 *The Abominable Snowman (Ostroznie Yeti)*
    d: Andrzej Csekalski

643 1961 *Samson*
   d: Andrzej Wajda

644 1961 *The Fat and the Lean* (*Le Gros et le Maigre*) as Servant
   d: Roman Polanski

645 1967 *The Fearless Vampire Killers* as Alfred
   d: Roman Polanski

646 1970 *The Magic Christian* as Man Listening to Lady Singer
   d: Joseph McGrath

647 1972 *Weekend of a Champion* as Interviewer
   d: Frank Simon

648 1973 *What?* (*Che?*) as Mosquito
   d: Roman Polanski

649 1974 *Blood for Dracula* as A Villager
   d: Paul Morrissey

650 1974 *Chinatown* as Man with Knife
   d: Roman Polanski

651 1976 *The Tenant* (*Le Locataire*) as Trelkovsky
   d: Roman Polanski

RADIO PERFORMANCES

1949– Acted as a child star in radio performances (and in the Cracow
1953   Theatre) during the years immediately following the war.

WRITINGS

Books

652 1973 Polanski, Roman. *What?* New York: The Third Press-Joseph
      Okpaku Publishing Company.
      See No. 17.

Screenplays

653 1957 *Break Up The Dance* (*Rozbijemy Zabawe*)
      See No. 3.

654 1958 *Two Men And A Wardrobe* (*Dwaj Ludzie Z Szasa*)
      See No. 5.

655 1959 *The Lamp* (*Lampa*)
      See No. 6.

656 1959 *When Angels Fall* (*Gdy Spadaja Anioly*)
      See No. 7.

657 1961 *The Fat And The Lean* (*Le Gros et le Maigre*)
See No. 8.

658 1962 *Knife In The Water* (*Nóż W Wodzie*)
See No. 9.

659 1962 *Mammals* (*Ssaki*)
See No. 10.

660 1963 *The Beautiful Swindlers* (*Les Plus Belles Escroqueries Du Monde*, Episode: "A River of Diamonds")
See No. 11.

661 1964 *A Taste For Women* (*Aimez-Vous Les Femmes?*)
Discovery of a corpse in a vegetarian restaurant by Jerome Fenouic, children's story writer, leads to his involvement in a series of bizarre adventures and the eventual arrests of gangs of feuding cannibal sects and opium smugglers.

662 1965 *Repulsion*
See No. 12.

663 1966 *Cul-De-Sac*
See No. 13.

664 1967 *The Fearless Vampire Killers*
See No. 14

665 1968 *Rosemary's Baby*
See No. 15.

666 1969 *A Day At The Beach*
"Uncle Bernie" and his friend, a small girl in a leg brace, spend a long, rainy day at the beach in which Bernie drinks himself into eventual collapse while his behavior disintegrates.

667 1971 *Macbeth*
See No. 16.

668 1973 *What?* (*Che?*)
See No. 17.

669 1976 *The Tenant* (*Le Locataire*)
See No. 19.

ASSISTANT DIRECTOR

670 1960 *Bad Luck*
d: Andrzej Munk
asst d: Roman Polanski

FILM PRODUCER

671 1969 *A Day at the Beach*
d: Simon Hesera
p: Roman Polanski

672 1972 *Weekend of a Champion*
d: Francis Simon
p: Roman Polanski

OPERA DIRECTOR

673 1974 *Lulu*
d: Roman Polanski

Archival Sources for Further Research

CALIFORNIA

674 Academy of Motion Picture Arts and Sciences
8949 Wilshire Boulevard
Beverly Hills, California 90211
Telephone: (213) 278–4313

Margaret Herrick Library
    Biography files of general articles and portrait stills on Polanski
    General script collection holds script from *Rosemary's Baby*.
    Paramount Collection holds still book and loose stills from *Rosemary's Baby*.
    Production files of reviews, programs and stills of Polanski films.

    Open to researchers Monday, Tuesday, Thursday, Friday, 9:00 a.m.
        to 5:00 p.m.

675 American Film Institute
501 Doheny Road
Beverly Hills, California 90210
Telephone: (213) 278–8777

Charles K. Feldman Library
    Transcript of Roman Polanski Seminar of March 20, 1974
    Biography file of clippings and articles on Polanski

    Open on a non-circulating basis to researchers Monday-Friday,
        9:00 a.m. to 5:30 p.m.

676 University of Southern California
University Park
Los Angeles, California 90007
Telephone: (213) 746–6058

University Library
Taped interview on *Rosemary's Baby* from March 13, 1969, discussion in Arthur Knight's class
Scripts of *The Fearless Vampire Killers* and *Rosemary's Baby*.

Materials for use on the premises

DISTRICT OF COLUMBIA

677 Reference Librarian
Library of Congress
Annex Building, Room 1046
Washington, D.C. 20540
Telephone: (202) 426-5840

Motion Picture Section
Holds copies of *The Fearless Vampire Killers, Rosemary's Baby, Macbeth* and *Chinatown* with descriptive material (pressbook, synopsis, clippings)

Researchers must make an appointment for the use of reference facilities; open Monday-Friday, 8:30 a.m. to 4:30 p.m.

NEW YORK

678 Museum of Modern Art
11 West 53 Street
New York, New York 10019
Telephone: (212) 956-6100
Study Center: (212) 956-4212

Study Center of the Department of Film
Clippings file holds reviews, articles on Polanski
Holds print of *Knife in the Water*

Researchers must make an appointment for use of the facilities; proof of validity of research from editor or instructor necessary. Open Monday-Friday, 1:00 p.m. to 5:00 p.m.; service fee for viewing films which must be booked at least one week in advance.

GERMANY (WEST)

679 Deutsches Institut fur Filmkunde
6202 Wiesbaden-Blebrich
Schloss, Germany
Telephone: 69074-75

Newspaper clippings file on Polanski
Stills and portrait stills of Polanski

Researchers should contact Eberhard Spiess, Deputy Director of the Institute, in advance as regards use of their resources.

680 Stiftung Deutsche Kinemathek
1000 Berlin 19
Pommernalle 1, Germany
Telephone: 3036–233 and 3036–234

Deutsche Film-und Fernsehakademie Berlin Library
German newspaper and trade-paper clippings
Stills, German press books and program leaflets on Polanski films

Materials for use on the premises

POLAND

681 Filmoteka Polska
Ul. Pulawska 61
00–975 Warszawa
Skr. Poczt. 65, Poland

Documentation Department
Extensive film reviews and articles on Polanski from Polish journals
Scripts and related materials from *Three Stories, The Enchanted Bicycle, A Generation, Wrecks, Phone My Wife, Lotna, See You Tomorrow, Innocent Sorcerers, The Abominable Snowman, Bad Luck, Samson, Knife in the Water, The Beautiful Swindlers, Repulsion, Cul-De-Sac, Macbeth*
Stills from *Three Stories, A Generation, Wrecks, Phone My Wife, Lotna, Innocent Sorcerers, The Abominable Snowman, Bad Luck, Samson, Knife in the Water, The Beautiful Swindlers, Repulsion, Cul-De-Sac, Macbeth, Chinatown*
Prints of all films made by Polanski in Poland

Materials for use on the premises; printed sources may be xeroxed on an exchange basis.

682 Panstowa Wyzsza Szkola Teatralna Filmowe
Ul. Targova 61
Lodz, Poland

Prints of all early student films Polanski made at the Polish National Film School

Distributors of Roman Polanski's Films

683 Creative Film Society
14558 Valerio Street
Van Nuys, Calfornia 91405

684 *Two Men and a Wardrobe*

685 Films Incorporated
1144 Wilmette Avenue
Wilmette, Illinois 60091
and
733 Green Bay Road
Wilmette, Illinois 60091

686 *Chinatown*

687 *The Fearless Vampire Killers*

688 *Rosemary's Baby*

689 *The Tenant*

690 Janus Film Library
745 Fifth Avenue
New York, New York 10023

691 *Knife in the Water*

692 MacMillan/Audio-Brandon
34 MacQuestern Parkway
Mount Vernon, New York 10550

693 *Cul-De-Sac*

694 Swank Motion Pictures
201 South Jefferson Avenue
St. Louis, Missouri 63166

695 *Macbeth*

696 *Repulsion*

Films Not Available Through Distribution:

Film Index

(All references pertain to entry numbers)

Author Index

(All references pertain to entry numbers)